BOOKS BY ROBERT LOWELL

The Oresteia of Aeschylus (1978)

Day by Day (1977)

Selected Poems (1976)

The Dolphin (1973)

History (1973)

For Lizzie and Harriet (1973)

Notebook (1969) (Revised and expanded edition, 1970)

Prometheus Bound (1969)

The Voyage & other versions of poems by Baudelaire (1969)

Near the Ocean (1967)

The Old Glory (1965)

For the Union Dead (1964)

Imitations (1961)

Phaedra (translation) (1961)

Life Studies (1959)

The Mills of the Kavanaughs (1951)

Lord Weary's Castle (1946)

Land of Unlikeness (1944)

THE ORESTEIA OF AESCHYLUS

ROBERT LOWELL

THE ORESTEIA
OF AESCHYLUS

FARRAR · STRAUS · GIROUX

New York

Library of Congress Cataloging in Publication Data
Aeschylus.   /   The oresteia of Aeschylus.
CONTENTS: Agamemnon.—Orestes.—The furies.
I.   Lowell, Robert.   II.   Title.
PA3827.A7L6   882'.01   78-9863

I do not want to cry down my translation of Aeschylus, but to say what I've tried to do and not tried. I have written from other translations, and not from the Greek. One in particular, Richmond Lattimore's, has had my admiration for years, it is so elaborately exact. I have aimed at something else: to trim, cut, and be direct enough to satisfy my own mind and at a first hearing the simple ears of a theater audience.

No version of the *Oresteia*, even a very great one, such as Marlowe or Milton might have written, can be anything like what was performed first in Athens with music, dance, masks, and an audience of thirty thousand or more—an event we cannot recover and something no doubt grander than any play we can see.

R. L.

CONTENTS

A NOTE ON THE TEXT

Lowell hoped his version of the *Oresteia* could be performed in one evening. *Agamemnon* and *Orestes* were written in the early 1960's; *The Furies* was added in the last year of his life, for a projected production of the entire trilogy at Lincoln Center. (*The Furies*, begun during December 1976, was finished by the end of the following January.[1]) It wasn't produced. Lincoln Center decided to do *Agamemnon* alone, in the uncut translation of Edith Hamilton.

So Lowell never saw his version performed. The text never underwent the revision and reshaping that *Prometheus Bound*, for example, received when he worked with Jonathan Miller (and others), at Yale in 1967. When he returned to Harvard from England at the end of January 1977, with the manuscript of *The Furies*, he was ill—and eager to finish his new book of poems, *Day by Day*. He spent the spring rewriting *Day by Day*, and the summer working on an essay, "New England and Further."

When Lowell died, the *Oresteia* had never (so far as I know) been subjected to that characteristic, open process of discussion and argument and revision, which he gave every manuscript that he saw through the press.

What follows is a reading version of the text. In every case, I have tried to incorporate the numerous handwritten marginal revisions.[2] The revisions increase with each play. I hope that someday a critical edition will appear; but I'm certain that Lowell would have wanted the *Oresteia*—at least at first—to exist without "a litter of variants."

Frank Bidart

---

[1] Lowell attempted *The Furies* when he translated the other two plays, but after four pages abandoned it. (See the Appendix for an excerpt from this version.)

[2] My aim has been a conservative text, based on Lowell's manuscript practice. This practice—his manner of indicating revisions, etc.— was idiosyncratic, but essentially consistent. I have not regularized or "normalized" punctuation, capitalization or other details, except where Lowell clearly would have done so (e.g., the typography of stage directions). In the passages (few, and minor) where alternative solutions are possible, none significantly alters the sense.

AGAMEMNON

Characters

WATCHMAN

CHORUS OF OLD MEN

CLYTEMNESTRA

HERALD

AGAMEMNON

CASSANDRA

AEGISTHUS

SLAVE WOMEN

GUARD OF AEGISTHUS

AGAMEMNON

[Scene: a space in front of the palace of Agamemnon in Argos. Night. A WATCHMAN *on the roof of the palace]*

WATCHMAN

I've lain here a year,
crouching like a dog on one elbow,
and begged the gods to end my watch.
I've watched the stars. I know their comings
and goings, the bringers of winter and the bringers
of summer. The stars burn with power,
and rule their empty spaces like kings.

But I'm no star-gazer. Clytemnestra
stationed me here to wake her when the beacon
shall flame in the east proclaiming Troy
has fallen. She has the mind of a man.
She set my bed on the roof of Atreus.
Its statues spy on me, I'm rotted by mildew,
I can't sleep, I can't dream, my only vision
is bodiless fear. If I start humming   *[Tries to hum
to stay awake, my mouth dries,   and cannot]*
my heart stops, and I think of this house
where nothing runs with its old grandeur.

I must say my futile, nightly prayer:
"Zeus, end my watch, light up the beacon,
destroy Troy." Nothing will happen.

[*Pause. A light appears, gradually increasing, the light of
the beacon*]

What am I seeing? The sky's on fire.
I must run and call the Queen.
There'll be shouting and dancing in the streets.
She will lead the dancers through Argos.
Troy's down, Troy's burning!
The dice have fallen right for my King.

Agamemnon is returning. I shall grasp his hand,
but I've nothing to say to him.
A black ox stands on my tongue.
I have a story I can only tell
someone who knows already. Say nothing—
this house would speak if it had a tongue!

[*Exit* WATCHMAN. *Enter* CHORUS OF OLD MEN. *The day begins
to dawn*]

[*New scene. More light. Palace now visible. Music to start
Chorus*]

LEADER OF CHORUS

Ten years have passed since Menelaus
and Agamemnon, kings from God,
double thrones, double scepters,
gathered the fighting men of Greece,
and marched them on a thousand ships.
They were like eagles screaming with bloodlust,

beating the mile-high air, circling
back and forth, back and forth,
over the nest of their choked young.

Some idle god, Apollo or Zeus,
heard the harsh cries of the birds, and gave them
his fury. They fell from the sky on Troy.

Thousands have died there for one loose woman.
Legs break, knees grind
in the dust, the wounded are killed without mercy.
Greek and Trojan have the same luck.
Things are what they are. Neither
burnt-flesh, oil, tears nor blood
satisfy the thirst of the gods.

We were too old for the army. My King
left me here to hobble on my stick,
and drop like a withered leaf in the heat.
A child would make a better spearman.

[CLYTEMNESTRA *crosses the stage. The* CHORUS *continues*]

SECOND VOICE

Lady, Clytemnestra, Queen
of Argos, tell us what to do.
What have you heard? Why do you order
sacrifices to all the gods
of our city? Oblations are burning to the powers
of the sky, the herds and the market-place.
Are these your orders? May the drugging incense

of the royal oil give us peace.
May hope shine in the bright flames,
and dispel the dark, insatiable
meditation that eats my heart.

LEADER OF CHORUS

I know the omen of the angry birds
hurled Agamemnon and Menelaus
like a spear at Troy—two thrones, one mind!
Two eagles came to our kings,
one white-tailed, the other black.
They lit on the spear-hand side of the palace.
Everyone saw them. They killed a hare.
Her unborn young were bursting from her side.
Cry death, cry death, but may the good prevail.

Then Calchas, the prophet of the army, cried:
"The eagles are the sons of Atreus feasting
on the hare. In time our armament
shall fall on Troy, and butcher its rich
herds of people, but let us fear
the gods lest they loosen the iron claw.
There's a goddess, who
is sick of the eagles' banquet. She pities
the unborn young and the shivering mother."
Cry death, cry death, but may the good prevail.

SECOND VOICE

Glory to Zeus, whatever he is:
he cut off the testicles of his own father,
and taught us dominion comes from pain!

LEADER OF CHORUS

Then the winds died. For weeks, the sulking
fleet stuck to shores of Aulis.
Ropes, sails, hulls rotted.
Stagnation spoiled the flower of Argos.
Minds broke, men starved.
Calchas, the prophet of the army, cried:
"The death of a girl will free the winds.
Iphigenia, the King's daughter, must die."

THIRD VOICE

Then Agamemnon smashed his staff
on the ground. He wept, saying, "The gods
will curse me if I disobey this order.
I shall be cursed if I murder my child,
the love of my house, and stain my hands
with her blood at the altar. Whatever I do
will destroy me. How can I betray
my ships and lose faith in the war?
My soldiers are mutinous. They cry for winds,
and care nothing for the blood of a child.
The winds must blow. May all be well."

FOURTH VOICE

When the King accepted this necessity,
he grew evil. Crosswinds darkened
his mind, his will stopped at nothing.
It pleased him to imagine the infatuation
of his hard heart was daring and decision.
Agamemnon wanted his ships to sail,
he was willing to kill his own daughter
to avenge the adultery of his brother's wife.

FIFTH VOICE

"Father, help me," she cried, but her terror
meant nothing to the kings in their impatience for the battle.
Her father spoke the solemn prayers,
and ordered the priests to lift his child
like a goat above the altar. Her robes
fluttered like feathers, then she lay there fainting.
Her father made them gag her lovely mouth.
He was afraid she would curse this house.

SIXTH VOICE

Her saffron robe fell to the ground.
She looked with pity at her familiar killers,
as if she were seated at the banquet table,
and wanted to call the guests by their names
before she lifted the third cup,
and sang with her weak, clear voice
in honor of her father.

I will not talk of what happened next.
I didn't see it. The ships sailed.

SECOND VOICE

The future will be plain when it comes.
The killer will be killed.

[CLYTEMNESTRA *enters again*]

THIRD VOICE

We pray fortune to smile on the Queen's
desires. She is our city's protector.

[CHORUS *turns to* CLYTEMNESTRA]

LEADER OF CHORUS

We have come, Clytemnestra, to honor you.
It's proper for us to obey our Queen,
when the King is gone and the throne empty.
Have you heard good news, or is it only
hope that makes you light the altars?
We would gladly hear you, but accept your silence.

CLYTEMNESTRA

You shall hear more joy than you ever hoped for.
We are watching the dawn rising
from its mother, the night. The Greeks are in Troy.

CHORUS

What are you saying?

CLYTEMNESTRA

We have taken Troy. Am I speaking clearly?

CHORUS

A slow delight steals over me,
I am weeping with joy, but what are your proofs?

CLYTEMNESTRA

The word of a god.

CHORUS

Did the god send you a dream?

CLYTEMNESTRA

I don't believe in dreams.

CHORUS

But you spoke of a god.

CLYTEMNESTRA

You ask me wearisome questions.
Do you think you are talking to a young girl?

CHORUS

Tell us when the city fell.
Who told you? How did he get here   [*Several*
so quickly? Who was your messenger?   *voices*]

CLYTEMNESTRA

The god of fire. The first fire
was Troy going down in ruin.
Then beacon after beacon took fire.
Mount Ida took it, then the flame raced
to the horn of Hermes on Lemnos, then it scaled
the blank rock face of Zeus at Athos.
It towered skyward, and overarched
the ocean's shoulders. Pine timbers
crackled into gold like the noonday sun.
The fire climbed the heights of Macistus—
it was like a winning runner or the herald of light.
It didn't sleep. It straddled the Euripus,
struck Messapion. There my watchman heaped
up stacks of heather, evergreen branches,
pyramids of caulked barrels.
Like the harvest moon, it rolled over
the Asopus river valley to Cithaeron.
There my men built an even higher
warning beacon than I had commanded.
It whitened the staring bog of Gorgopis,
ignited the crags of Aegyplanctus,

then galloping westward to me, it passed
the Saronic Strait, and set off our watchtower
here on the Arachnian Rock. Look,   [*Points to*
a light has fallen on the House of Atreus.   *torch on the*
I made this chain of beacons. I chose   *roof*]
each watchman. Agamemnon's in Troy. My husband
is sending me this message of fire.

CHORUS

The gods shall hear our prayers of thanksgiving,
but I should like to listen until
all wonder fades. Is Agamemnon returning?

CLYTEMNESTRA

The Greeks are sacking Troy. Listen,
I can almost hear its death-cries.
Pour vinegar and oil in one bowl,
you would not say they mixed in friendship.
The conquerors and conquered have different voices.
The Trojans are howling by the stripped bodies
of their loved ones stacked like wood in the streets.
By the auction blocks, children in chains
weep for the old parents who begot them.
But the Greeks have work before breakfast.
They are marauding in gangs through the city.
There's no discipline. Orders are laughed at.
Each man moves by chance.
They are at home in the Trojan houses.
No more mud, no more rain,
no more camping in the open by their ships,
no more kings, no more sentries!

They sleep all night.
All that Troy had is ours.

They are inhuman from ten years in the field,
but let them dread the gods of the city,
and spare the temples. Let no lust
seize these men to violate what they must not.
Our ships must still run the homeward stretch.
A great storm is gathering. Even if our soldiers
return safely, I think the anger
of those we killed may never sleep.
Oh let us do no more harm!

Old men, I have spoken my fears to you
like a woman, but may the good prevail.

CHORUS

You have spoken like a man and our protector.
Queen of Argos,
we will begin our prayer to the gods.
The war was worth what it cost.

[CLYTEMNESTRA *goes back into the palace. Music*]

Oh Zeus, our God and our darkness,   [*Different
giver of beauty and power,   voices chant
you cast out a binding net   the stanzas*]
that caught the towers of Troy.
How slowly, how carefully, you stretched
the cord that killed that city!

Paris caused the war. He turned
to blackness like a forged coin

rung and rejected on the touchstone.
He was like a child trying
to net the skimming swallow.
He trampled on the delicacy of things.

Paris seduced Helen,
the wife of his friend and host,
Helen, our Clytemnestra's sister.
She danced lightly through the gates
of Troy, daring beyond
daring. Her dowry was death.

She came to the Trojans with a clash
of shields, the galley was sinking
with plunder; her dowry was death.
We weep for the champions of the bed.
Netted together, they saw
splendor, but only in a dream.

Our own fields are unworked.
Two generations have fed
the conscription of King Agamemnon.
He is a money-changer of bodies.
He took our lovely children
and changed them to dust in the urns.

Each new ship brought us a cargo
of urns. We wept and said:
"They were good at dying, but they died
for another man's wife."

How many rot far off
in the Asia they hated and conquered!

Glory to Zeus, the sure marksman!
His arrows neither drop short,
nor fly up to the stars. Here,
men curse the House of Atreus,
they curse the King and his war.
Their voices are thick with hatred.

*[This stanza
should be sung
by the First
Voice and with
the same music]*

The black Furies lurk here
in this hooded night. They stalk
a man fortunate beyond
the limits of mercy. They wrench
him to darkness. Among the ciphers,
he has no pleasure in power.

I ask for my own house and field.
I ask for nothing men
could envy me. I do
not want to plunder cities.
I do not want to be taken,
and die in the chains of a slave.

FIRST VOICE

All Argos is burning with victory torches.

*[Various
members of the
Chorus, speaking
one by one]*

SECOND VOICE

Who knows what happened?

THIRD VOICE

The gods may have lied to us.

FOURTH VOICE

It's like a woman to be hysterical
with conviction before she knows the facts.

SECOND VOICE

She was trying to dazzle and blind us
with her chain of flickering and flashing beacons.

THIRD VOICE

Everything flickers and flashes in her mind.

FOURTH VOICE

Someone's coming.

FIRST VOICE

A herald is running up from the beach.
His head is circled with olive shoots.
I can see by the dust on his sandals
he has come from the army without stopping.
At last we have an eyewitness
and a man, not a pile of pine-timbers
puffing out smoke-signals.
He has come from Agamemnon, he will tell us
if Troy has fallen . . . Or else . . . No, Troy's
fallen. I want to believe it.

SECOND VOICE

It's treason to disbelieve in the fall of Troy.

HERALD

Soil of Argos, earth of my fathers,
on this bright day of the tenth year,
I come back. I left with ignorant expectations—
I have lost them all; one was true.
I shall die in Argos, my beloved country.
Glory to Zeus, glory to our sunlight—

[*Speaking formally,
as if he had
memorized his
words. From time
to time, he makes
solemn gestures
to the Chorus,
audience and
palace*]

I greet the gods of our market-place,
you above all, my road-friend, Hermes,
the lovely herald and patron of heralds.
May the spirits of the dead accept the survivor
who was spared by the spear. Roof of our palace,
hall of our kings, House of Atreus,
may your tribal gods who face the sun
look down with bright eyes on our King.
After ten years, Agamemnon is returning
like the heat of summer to this cold land.
He fought in our lines like a soldier. Welcome him.
He is the man who smashed Troy,
and buried the Trojans with the shovel of Zeus.
Their fields are scorched. Their houses are rubble.
Their seed has been wiped out from Asia.
Welcome, Agamemnon.
Now neither Paris, nor his people shall boast
that the atonement was less than the crime.
They were house-breakers, pirates and rapists,
they have lost Helen, who caused the war,
their city, and even the dirt it stood on.

CHORUS

Hail and be glad, herald of the army.

HERALD

I am home. I am weeping for happiness.
I no longer ask the gods for death.

CHORUS

We are weeping with you.

HERALD

Did you long for us, as we longed for our homes?

CHORUS

We no longer ask the gods for death.

HERALD

You asked for death! Was there someone you feared
while Agamemnon was away fighting?

CHORUS

We are not Trojans. We are still alive.

HERALD

Well, we won the war and saved our city.   [*Confidential
It took time, some of our King's plans   tone*]
worked, others didn't.
It's all one, we were Greek soldiers, not the gods.
I could talk about the hard work of sailing—
day and night, the heavy oar
ram-rodding back, ram-rodding ahead,
bodies flattened like salt fish in a barrel,
the rollers, the vomit. Asia was worse—
we intrenched below the Trojan walls,
mud slopped up water from the mountain,
lice scissored through our groins, clean,
protected men skewered us with their arrows.
One winter even the seagulls died.
They floated like blocks of ice. Next summer,
the lazy sea would slacken at noon.
It slept and steamed in the dead heat.

We are not forced to relive the war.
Its ten years are gone for us,
and gone for those who died. They rest
from our defeats and rallies, and care for nothing.
Here in the sunlight of Greece, we boast:
"This is Argos, the destroyer of Troy."

CHORUS

Troy is taken. I was uncertain at first,
but I am not too old to learn.
Go tell our Queen. She believed when we doubted.

[CLYTEMNESTRA, *who has been listening to the* HERALD's
speech in the background, comes forward]

CLYTEMNESTRA

I never doubted. I began our cry
of triumph on the confused night, when the first
beacon heralded the death of Troy.
Men laughed at me, saying, "You are dazzled
by your beacons. You believe Troy has fallen.
How can a woman be so lighthearted?"
They thought I was wandering in my mind,
but like a woman I lighted the altars,
and kept on believing. Voice after voice
caught up my cry: "Troy has fallen."

[CLYTEMNESTRA *turns to the* HERALD]
There's no need
for you to tell me your long story,
I shall soon hear the truth from my husband.
I am ready. I am restless. Nothing's sweeter

for a wife than the first embrace of her captain
returning safe in God's hand.
Tell Agamemnon to hurry to his beloved.
Here he shall find a wife as loyal
as when he left her, the watchdog of his house,
true to her master, but a wolf to the intruder.
I have been faithful in all things,
I have broken no promise. For ten years,
I have known no pleasure with man.

[CLYTEMNESTRA *goes back into the palace*]

HERALD

Agamemnon is blessed in his wife.
She speaks like a queen, and tells the truth.

CHORUS

Clytemnestra has spoken. A clever
interpreter finds the true meaning
of a woman's words. But tell us what has happened
to our fleet. Is Menelaus, our King's
brother, alive and returning with Helen?

HERALD

We lost sight of King Menelaus and his ship.

CHORUS

Where is the rest of the fleet?

HERALD

We have lost the fleet.

CHORUS

Where is the army? Where are our sons?

HERALD

No man can tell you, only the sun,
the all-seeing and giver of life,
knows where they are. I wished to give my city
a single day to rejoice in the ruin
of Troy and Agamemnon's preservation . . .
All night the sea kept rising, wave
over black wave. Rain from Thrace
rattled through our rigging, oars snapped,
hulls splintered, we wallowed sidewise,
our bronze beaks rammed our own ships,
as we spun in the hand of an angry shepherd.
Then the sun came up. We could see
the blue Aegean blossom with bodies,
oars, timbers, figureheads—
a whole dead army on the sea.
Our ship kept floating. We lived.
Some god, no mortal, had handled our helm,
and saved us from the big sea, and led us
through the crooked, covered rocks of the channels.
We stared at the watery white sky,
and wept for our friends. If any were still
alive, they thought of us as dead.
I think of them as dead.

CHORUS

What happened to Helen who caused the war?

HERALD

I don't know.

(*Exit* HERALD)

CHORUS

FIRST VOICE

Helen, Clytemnestra's sister,
was well-named, a hell to men,
a hell to many cities,
a hell to the Greek fleet.
Two hundred galleys sailed
with Agamemnon. One is returning.

SECOND VOICE

Helen, the wife of Menelaus,
came as a dying wind
and windless lull to Troy—
her marriage was death.

THIRD VOICE

The Trojans carried a lion
cub like a kitten into their house.
It played with the children, and was petted
like a bright-eyed child,
always laughing with hunger.
They fed it their daughter's milk.

FOURTH VOICE

Helen was the sister of Clytemnestra.
She grew up. She prowled like a lioness
through the houses of the Trojans.
She was true to her blood and breeding.

FIRST VOICE

Our forefathers believed that wealth
and high fortune never
come to a good end.

SECOND VOICE

I disbelieve our forefathers. I say the gods
punish none but the wicked.

THIRD VOICE

I say the houses
of the just have merciful heirs.

FOURTH VOICE

Righteousness shines only
in the smoke of the poor man's house.

FIRST VOICE

I do not want
the power of a king, or his purple
stained with a daughter's blood.

[*Enter* AGAMEMNON *with* CASSANDRA *beside him in his chariot.
The Old Men want to warn Agamemnon somehow, but they
have many difficulties. They don't know whether he is their
old, familiar, patriarchal king, or some frightening despot,
almost a monster and someone of another species. They are
full of apprehensions, but are uncertain and fear Clytemnestra*]

Hail, Agamemnon!

SECOND VOICE

Hail, king of kings,
Son of Atreus, captain of the Greek armies.

THIRD VOICE

We welcome you, destroyer of Troy.

FIRST VOICE

Oh how shall I honor you, my King?
You are not a tyrant. You are our father.
You trust your children to tell you the truth.

SECOND VOICE

I will neither hold back,
nor fly too high. I despise the flatterer,
who plays at being unhappy with the unhappy,
yet never feels the tooth of sorrow at his heart.

THIRD VOICE

I will not twist my face in false smiles
to lull the man of unfaltering will.

FIRST VOICE

I can only tell you what you know already.

SECOND VOICE

You are the shepherd of Argos, you know your flock.

THIRD VOICE

The eyes of men cannot lie to you.

FIRST VOICE

I will not hide the truth from you,
my King. You were ugly to me and almost
an outlaw, when you gathered your army.
You swore you would bring back Helen,
even if you bled your city to death.

SECOND VOICE

You abandoned your city. You took
our sons, and sent us empty urns.
But now we welcome you, Agamemnon.
You are our good King. You've won the war.
You are home. Our troubles are gladness.

THIRD VOICE

When you search through the city, you will learn
who stood by you, and who were the deserters.

AGAMEMNON

First I salute Argos and our gods.
They have worked long to bring me home,
and hardened my will to level Troy.
The gods were my partners. They did not falter,
or talk like a woman. With one voice,
they threw their votes in the urn of blood,
saying, "Troy and its sons must die."
A hand dangled a moment over
the urn of mercy, but no vote dropped.
Troy is gone. Its sky is a smoke-cloud,
the live ash stinks with the savor of its riches.
For this, we must give thanks to the gods and their justice.
They entangled the city in the net of my fury.
Because one Greek woman was raped,
a beast, the lion of Argos, broke
the Trojans, and lapped the blood of their kings.

I have offered my solemn thanks to the gods.
Now, old men of Argos, I will hear you.
I know your hidden thoughts.
The eyes of men cannot lie to me.
What you are thinking is true.

*[He is a
contradictory
character,
kindly yet
terrifying, a
natural ruler,
very practised
and alert at it,
yet invincibly
and almost
willfully
blinded to
his danger]*

[*Pause. In the brief silence, it almost seems as if Agamemnon
had intuited the plot against his life. When he speaks, it is
obvious that he is off the track*]

Few
men have the character to accept another's
good fortune. Most are sick with their own weakness,
they chatter with anguish, when a friend succeeds.
I speak with knowledge. I could give names,
many of them were kings and my soldiers—
Everyone failed me. Only Odysseus,
who sailed unwillingly, was wise and obeyed.
I praise this one man. But is he alive?

Obedient to the laws of the gods and Argos,
we will proclaim a full assembly
of our citizens. In our ten years' absence,
many things have fallen from grandeur.
That was to be expected; your queen
has done what she could, a woman's best.
We will examine everything,
discuss everything, mend everything.
Some things are diseased, some are healthy.
We promise we will not hesitate
to probe, burn and use the knife
to cure our corruption. Rejoice, old men,
you are ruled by a king!

[CLYTEMNESTRA *is seen in the palace, as the doors open*]

I must enter the palace of Atreus, my father.
I will pray to his gods. They sent me out,
they have brought me home. I will wash off my blood.

[CLYTEMNESTRA *comes forward. She looks boldly at* AGA-
MEMNON, *then turns aside and speaks to him at first by
addressing the* CHORUS]

CLYTEMNESTRA

Old men, I am not ashamed to stand
before you and show my love for my husband.
I am older than when he left. I've lost
my shyness. Even modesty decays.

Your city went on living and prospered—
I speak of my own unlivable life
of monotonous impotence, when he was gone.
I have sat here without a husband.
Trapped, terrified, beaten down,
I lived on the rumors of Greek defeats.
I have given audience to runner on the heels
of runner, each with worse news.
Men proclaimed him dead, they proclaimed him alive;
he died and recovered, and recovered to die.
If Agamemnon had suffered one
death-stab in twenty, his poor body
would have been gashed into holes like a fishnet.
I tried to kill myself.
My handmaidens cut me down from a beam.
They unknotted a rope from my neck.

Agamemnon!
You are looking for your son, Orestes.
He should be standing here to receive you.
I sent him away. Do not be angry with me.
Strophius, the Phocian, was my advisor. Each day,
I expected your army would collapse at Troy.
I feared this abandoned people would revolt,

and mob our palace and kill your son.
It is men's nature, Agamemnon,
to trample on the man who has failed them!

Do you see these old men? They are weeping
for joy. They know I haven't failed you.
I myself cannot weep.
I lost that comfort when I was sitting out
the nights crying for you, and straining
to see the beacons that never flamed.
I slept for minutes, but the thinnest whirring
of a gnat's wing woke me. I dreamed.
In my dreams I saw you wounded by the Trojans.
They always killed you. How often, I held you,
coughing out your life-blood in my arms!
My minutes of sleep were months of fighting.

[*She turns for a moment from* AGAMEMNON *to the* CHORUS]

Now my suffering is over. I hail
this man. He is the watchdog of the house of Atreus,
the oak pole that props the palace,
land to the drowning sailor, the keel
that steadies our ship, daybreak that saves
our fleet from the night of wrecks.

[*She turns to* AGAMEMNON *and comes nearer to him*]

                            Oh fresh

running brook, I run to you.
I will never stop drinking.
It's sweet to escape from necessity.

My Beloved, come down to me from your chariot,
but your foot that trampled on Troy
must not touch the earth of Argos.

[SLAVE WOMEN *come forward with piles of crimson tapestries*]

My maidens, why are you delaying?
Cover the ground for Agamemnon.
He will come to us on tapestries.
He will enter a house he despaired of seeing.
He will walk the crimson cloths of justice.
Leave the rest to my sleepless mind.

God help me, I've done what had to be done.

[*Clytemnestra's* SLAVES *spread out the tapestries, and begin
to bow and wail before* AGAMEMNON]

AGAMEMNON

I humbly thank you for the management of my household,
Daughter of Leda. Your welcome oration
matched my absence . . . it was too long.
More suitable praise will be spoken by men.

Stop this crawling on the ground, and howling
like wolves at me! I won't be softened.
I am the king of a small Greek city,
not an Asiatic despot or Ethiopian headman.
My people would laugh at me, if they saw
me swaggering on these embroideries and spoiling them.
This is ritual for the gods. I am a man.
I insist on being honored as a man.
As long as I follow the laws of my kingdom,
the gods will preserve me.

CLYTEMNESTRA

Priam would have walked on the tapestries, if he'd won.

AGAMEMNON

Priam? He was a Trojan. He might well have walked on the cloths.

CLYTEMNESTRA

A great king rules by surrendering trifles.

AGAMEMNON

You never surrender. How can this thing
mean so much to you on the day of my return?
Who admires a wife for winning arguments?

CLYTEMNESTRA

My Beloved, you are smiling. You will humor my weakness.
You will walk on the tapestries.

AGAMEMNON

[AGAMEMNON *turns to* CASSANDRA]

I beg you to receive this girl with gentleness.
The gods look kindly on merciful masters,
for no one ever willingly became a slave.
She was a princess. Now she is our possession.

Peace, peace. You are the master for the moment.
I will walk on your cloths.
Call someone to loose my sandals. My sandals
are docile slaves, they serve my feet.

Ah Clytemnestra, may no god see me and strike me
from afar, when I enter my house. I will crush
the beauty of these tapestries stained crimson by the sea.

CLYTEMNESTRA

The sea is ours. Man will not exhaust it;
it gives us a green field for our ships,
and royal crimson to dye our clothes.
The house of Atreus rules the sea;
poverty cannot come near us.
How often, if the gods had wished it, I would
have woven and sacrificed a thousand
blood-red cloths to save your life.
For when the root is alive, the oak
will spread its leaves to shade the house.
The war is finished. The soldier's day
is over. Agamemnon, you bring us heat
in winter; and in the summer, when
the green vine leaves tremble
and bow to the earth with red grapes,
there will be coolness in our homes,
because the master rules his house.

Oh Zeus, fulfiller of prayers, answer me!
The ripe fruit is ready to fall.

> [AGAMEMNON *goes over the tapestries into the palace.*
> CLYTEMNESTRA *follows him. Two alternating voices of the*
> CHORUS, *one pathetically hopeful, the other ominous*]

CHORUS

FIRST VOICE

This is the full summer in Argos.
Agamemnon is home. I hear his voice.
Listen, a thousand summer sounds!

The house of Atreus can rest from labor,
all is ripe for the harvest.

SECOND VOICE

But why do I hear the insect Fear
beating its trapped wings in my heart?
I hear the grinding of a knife,
and the cry of a girl at the altar.
She was ripe for the harvest.

FIRST VOICE

Yet day followed day, ten years
have buried the bronze cables of the ships
in wave on wave of loose sand,
since Agamemnon and the army cast off
for the destruction of Troy.

SECOND VOICE

I have no hope. Crops rise and fall,
and summer follows on the heels of summer,
but when a man dies, and his black
blood falls at his feet,
no spell will sing him back.

[CLYTEMNESTRA *returns and speaks to* CASSANDRA. *She assumes an attitude of casual regal serenity, but has an air of impatience, anger and excitement*]

CLYTEMNESTRA

Cassandra, you may go to the palace now,
and stand with our other slaves at the altar.
When you are cleansed, you will enter our service.
Don't tremble. We are not adventurers or tyrants
suddenly enthroned by a throw of the dice.

We are an old house, we are used to slaves.
Whatever is customary shall be yours.

CHORUS

Clytemnestra has spoken clearly.
You must answer her, but perhaps you cannot.
We have heard your speech is the twitter of a swallow.

[*Throughout this scene with* CLYTEMNESTRA, CASSANDRA
stares at the ground and gives no sign of having heard a word]

CLYTEMNESTRA

Oh, she understands and will mind me.

CHORUS

Come, Cassandra, step down from the chariot.

CLYTEMNESTRA

Hurry. The sheep are bleating at the altar,
and stretching their throats to bless
this day we never hoped to see.
Make some sign to me with your hand,
if you cannot master our language.

CHORUS

I think she needs an interpreter.
She is still like a wild bird caught in our net.

CLYTEMNESTRA

She is still caught in her own wild thoughts.
Hasn't she just left her burning city?
She won't be handled by her destroyers, or take
the bit, until she bleeds at the mouth.
I'm not standing here to be stared at.

[CLYTEMNESTRA *strides back into the palace. The Leader of the* CHORUS *speaks kindly to* CASSANDRA, *but sometimes he seems so puzzled that he seems to be talking to himself*]

CHORUS

I am not angry. I pity you.
Come down, Cassandra, and leave your chariot.
You must pick up the yoke of a slave.

[CASSANDRA *steps down and faces a statue of Apollo*]

CASSANDRA

Oh, Oh, Apollo!

CHORUS

Why do you trouble Apollo with your grief?

CASSANDRA

Oh Apollo, Apollo!
Where have you led me? Whose house is this?

CHORUS

The house of Atreus. Surely, you must know.

CASSANDRA

No, no, this is a meathouse. God
hates these people. They have hung the flesh
of their own young on hooks.

CHORUS

She is like a dog picking up the blood-trail.

CASSANDRA

I see them. The small children are crying.
They are trying to push back the knife with their hands.

CHORUS

We know she is a prophet. We want no prophets.

CASSANDRA

The woman has the mind of a man.
What is she doing? What is she plotting?
Help is far away from the beloved.
He cannot be healed.

CHORUS

What is she trying to tell us now?

CASSANDRA

She is bathing the man who shares her bed.
She is holding . . . She is holding up a net.
She is fitting one hand. She is fitting his other.
She is the death-net who shares his bed . . .

No, look. Be quick. On guard there.
Pen the bull from the cow.
She has tossed a net on his horns.
Her black horn has gored him.
He is bloodying the water of his bath . . .

Apollo, Apollo, I am begging for my life.
Why have you brought me to the house of Atreus?
Why, why, except to die with him?

CHORUS

Cassandra, when you sing your death-song,
you are like the nightingale,
unsatisfied, forever

crying, *Itys, Itys,*
the name of the child she killed.

CASSANDRA

How I envy the nightingale,
when the nightingale died, the gods
gave her beating wings,
and a bird's life of song.
My life was, is,
and shall be the edge of the knife.

CHORUS

Tell us how you learned to sing in anguish.

CASSANDRA

I drank from the river of Troy.
I sang of the blood in the water.
Soon I will sing by the river of death.

CHORUS

A child could understand this.

CASSANDRA

Ah Troy, my city, the pitiful, munching
sheep my father slaughtered by your walls
were no help at all to save you!
I too with my brain on fire must die.

CHORUS

She talks of death and dying, as if some angry
power were kneeling down on her,
and crushing the life from her body.
She knows some truth. She is trying to warn us.
I cannot see the end.

CASSANDRA

No more circling, I'm on the scent.
I hear the choir of your Furies.
Do not try to conceal them from me.
They are established here as your closest friends.
They will not leave the house of Atreus.
Why did you nurse them with your own blood,
until nothing else could satisfy their thirst?
Listen, the menacing vibration of the voices
never relents. Your Furies curse
the kinsman who outraged his brother's bed.
Have I hit the mark? Have I drawn blood?

CHORUS

You have hit the mark. We marvel at how
you could come here from Troy, and know the truth.

CASSANDRA

I was taught by the God, Apollo.

CHORUS

Did you sleep with Apollo, and have children by him,
as people do?

CASSANDRA

I promised I would, but I broke my promise.

CHORUS

But you are still able to see the truth.

CASSANDRA

I tell the truth, but no one believes me.

CHORUS

We do.

CASSANDRA

I see the truth. I must tell the truth
that no one will see. No one believes me.

[*She points to the roof of the palace*]

Don't you see them playing on the roof?
So small and young? Our King's old playmates?
His little cousins?
They are the children killed by someone close to them.
They have filled their hands with their own flesh,
as if they would eat it. They are holding up
their own entrails for their father to eat.
Someone is preparing for vengeance. A whining
lion tumbles in the master's bed.

[*She stretches her head toward the door of the palace, as if she were calling Agamemnon*]

Oh Master—only
Agamemnon's slave can call you Master—
you had eyes in the back of your head, and you went
sleepless, when your killers were burning my city,
but do you know this bitch that pricks up
her ears and licks your fingers?
Your bitch! But she's not a coward. It takes
daring for the female to slaughter the male.
What shall I call her? She is Scylla,
the snake, the sea-bitch, the smothering mother
of sailors, uncoiling and writhing and singing,
when her victim crawls up the rock to her claws.

Old men, old men, it doesn't matter,
if anyone believes me. What will happen will happen.

CHORUS

When you speak of this bitch, of Scylla . . .
what do you mean?

CASSANDRA

You'll look on Agamemnon dead.

CHORUS

Don't say this. Pray and be silent.

CASSANDRA

I must pray? *They* do not pray.
They plan. They strike. They kill.

CHORUS

What man is planning to kill our King?

CASSANDRA

What *man!* Fools, you have understood nothing . . .

I tell you it's a woman-lioness. She beds
with the wolf while her husband is out in the field.
She will cut me down. Poor King, poor Mistress!
We will float like leaves in her bowl of poisons.

[*She holds out her priestly staff and garland, then throws
them to the ground*]

I hate this costume! My prophet's
staff, this string of flowers at my throat!
Down, break, damn you!

I have carried these emblems and wandered,
derided, starving and filthy past the houses
of my own people, who loved and hated me.
Now a stranger leads me here to die.
I am who I am.

But why am I weeping? I've seen my countrymen
die as they died. It's just the men
who killed us, should be killed in turn.
I will enter the house. We two must die,
then later a man shall die for the man,
and then the woman shall die for a woman.
Orestes, the homeless, will return and kill
the killers. I ask Clytemnestra
for a painless death.

CHORUS

Poor child, you have spoken long to us.
We have suffered less than you,
we are less wise than you.
Tell us why you linger here
so calmly, like a sheep to be killed?

CASSANDRA

I must die, strangers, I cannot escape.

CHORUS

You are so patient, because you are brave.

CASSANDRA

Only those about to die ever hear such praise.

[*She walks toward the gate of the palace, then starts back in horror*]

Terrifying to look in here, strangers!
The floor is heaped with bleeding bodies.

CHORUS

We only see
the innocent sacrificial sheep.

CASSANDRA

No, I see my open grave.
Good, I am going in. As I go,
I will weep for myself and Agamemnon.
We are through with our lives. Ah Friends,
do not imagine I am a wild bird,
fluttering and twittering with fear at a bush.

CHORUS

Poor Child, I pity you. You see
your death too clearly.

CASSANDRA

I do not wish to complain of my death.
What's life? At best, its sorrows are hardly
more pitiable than its joys. At worst,
one sweep of a wet sponge wipes out the picture.
Hear me. I call upon the sun.
May the sun shine down on our avengers,
and on the final merciful hour of their vengeance.
When they avenge Agamemnon, may they also
avenge a simple slave who died.
She was a small thing, and carelessly killed.

[CASSANDRA *goes into the palace. Members of the* CHORUS *cry
out the alternating stanzas*]

CHORUS

FIRST VOICE

Cassandra is standing with Agamemnon at the altar.
They are like a bride and bridegroom.

SECOND VOICE

He is the son of Atreus and the father
of Iphigenia.

THIRD VOICE

Must more blood
then be given for the generations who died?

AGAMEMNON   [*Shouting from inside the palace*]

I've been stabbed. Help me, I've been killed.

CHORUS

Someone's been stabbed in the palace.
Who's been killed? Who's calling us?

AGAMEMNON

I've been stabbed twice. Help me, I am dying.

CHORUS

Agamemnon has been killed. Let's do something.
How can we save him? How can we save ourselves?

FIRST VOICE

Call back the herald of the army.
He'll sound his trumpet, and assemble the people.

SECOND VOICE

No, rush the palace. We'll make the first rally.
We'll catch the assassins with their swords still wet.

THIRD VOICE

I'm with this man, he has my vote.
Smash the doors. Kill them with their own swords.

FOURTH VOICE

Why are we talking and debating here?
We'll have time to debate, when we're dead.

SECOND VOICE

Let's kill them.
We can't talk Agamemnon back to life.

THIRD VOICE

We'll hang them. This is just the beginning.
They are going to set up a tyranny in the city.

SECOND VOICE

Draw your swords. We'll kill them. I'd rather
die than live under the tyrants.

FOURTH VOICE

We'll die anyway under the tyrants.
I know them. They plan. They strike. They kill.

FIRST VOICE

No, wait. We must know what we are doing.
Did we see anyone die?

SECOND VOICE

We heard someone calling. We don't
even know if the voice was Agamemnon's.

[*The doors of the palace open.* CLYTEMNESTRA *comes out.
Cassandra's dead body is thrown in front of her, then
Agamemnon's is thrown on top of it*]

CLYTEMNESTRA

You see I have lied to you, and betrayed
your king. So be it. I unsay my lies.
How else could I trap the enemy, who killed
my child? How else could I build a fence
of nets too high for this beast to leap?
I have been training a long time for this match.
Now I've thrown him. I stand on the ground
where I struck him down. I deny nothing.
I threw out my net like a fisherman,
and caught him in an abundance of rich clothing.
He outguessed a hundred Trojan fighters,
but he could not move a finger, when I struck.

I stabbed twice. You heard him bellow.
His great legs couldn't help him.
When he fell, I struck him a third time,
out of joy and reverence for Zeus,
who rules the dead beneath the earth.
That's how he perished. When he vomited
his life out, the dark red blood rushed
like a summer shower, and splattered my hands.
I am glad. I stand up like a garden,
full of the first rain and bursting into flower.

Old men, I have told you the facts. Rejoice
with me, if you can, but I will glory.
If our religion allowed it, I would pour out wine
in thanksgiving on the dead man.
He brewed unpardonable evil for us.
Now he has drunk the cup.

CHORUS

How can you stand over your husband's body,
and boast of his murder?

CLYTEMNESTRA

Don't shout at me, as if I were
a cowardly woman. My heart will not tremble.
I am indifferent to your praise or blame.
You know this. I offer you Agamemnon,
dead, the work of this right hand.

CHORUS

What poison have you grubbed from the earth, or dragged
from the sea, Woman? You exult over
your husband you threw down and cut off.
You will be thrown down, you will be cut off,
you will be driven homeless from Argos.

CLYTEMNESTRA

Will you doom *me* to be driven from the city?
Will you damn *me* with the curse of the people?
Look at this dead man. You would not cross him,
when he looked over his fleecy flocks,
and picked out his own child, and slaughtered her
like a head of mutton. Your sons sailed.
They were soldiers, they should have hunted
Agamemnon like a destroyer from this land.
You and they did nothing. Now you condemn me.
I am ready. Break me by force,
if you can. If not, I'll break you.
You'll be taught, though late, to obey.

CHORUS

The blood on your hands has smeared your mind.
You will die friendless, you will be killed as you killed.

CLYTEMNESTRA

Listen, hear me. I offer the blood
of this man to the Furies of Iphigenia.
I shall never be afraid,
while Aegisthus, my loyal friend,
makes the fire shine at my hearth.
He is our shield of defiance. Now,
as always, he will stand beside us. But this man
cannot stand. Once his body
was the plaything of any girl in Troy,
now it lies smeared with the blood of this woman.
Cassandra saw wonders, she was wise at revelations,
she was quick to serve the rower at his bench.
Poor Swan, she sang her dying lamentation,
now heart to heart, she lies with her lover—
one blood!
The sight gives excitement to my own bed.

CHORUS

We lie on the slow bed of sickness.
We pray for sleep. We pray for death,
the sleep that lasts. Agamemnon, our shield,
our king, the kindest of men, is dead.
He was killed by his wife.

[*The dialogue
here becomes
less dramatic,
and more
formal and
ritualistic,
unrealistic,
musical,
harmonious*]

CLYTEMNESTRA

The sickness lies so deep in our blood,
no man or knife can reach the poison.

Three times we have washed the stain from our house.
When the old wound heals, it bleeds again,
but I do not pray for death.

CHORUS

Ah Helen, Oh scarlet rose,
you are stained with our blood.
Thousands of men have died for your return.
They rot at Troy.

CLYTEMNESTRA

Do not turn in your weak anger
on my sister, as if one woman could have killed
those multitudes of our bravest men.
This man assembled them. They screamed for winds,
and called for the blood of my child.

CHORUS

King, Oh my King, who will weep for you?
You slaughtered your child to save our city.
Now no one mourns you, no one will bury you.
You lie caught in the spider's web.
You were murdered by your wife.

CLYTEMNESTRA

I killed Agamemnon. I will bury Agamemnon,
but I cannot weep. Iphigenia, his child,
is waiting for him by the whirling river
of tears. Who else will kiss this father,
and hold him in her arms?

[AEGISTHUS *enters with his* GUARD, *who move with the efficient impersonality of a machine, and obviously come from another country*]

AEGISTHUS

Oh day of splendor, day of my freedom!
First I greet Argos and our gods.
The gods were my partners. They have pitied the helpless,
they have strangled this beast in the net of my fury.
My blood races with joy, when I see
this man at my feet. I could eat his heart.

CHORUS

Aegisthus, it's sinful to boast over the fallen.

AEGISTHUS

I vindicate my father. This man's
father, King Atreus, drove my father,
his own brother, Thyestes, from his home and kingdom.
My father might have been your king, but he gave way,
and then humbly came back as a suppliant.
Why shouldn't he have come back? He was loved here,
he was peaceful, he never polluted the doorstep
of a brother's house with its own blood.
Atreus didn't strike Thyestes. He kissed him,
he hung on his neck, he called for a feast
of thanksgiving, and sat him in the place of honor.
He even served him with his own hands,
he brought him fresh meat in a steaming dish.
The meat was chopped small. The hands,
feet and faces were carved away.
My father could not know what he was eating.
He ate his own children! When he knew,
he stumbled back, he choked out the meat,
he kicked the huge table over, cursing:
"May the whole house of Atreus crash to ruin!"

That's why Agamemnon is lying here.

[*Pause*]

It was I, I, I!
I was the third son of Thyestes. I was sent
into exile as a helpless, crying child.
Atreus and Agamemnon were afraid to kill me.
I pieced together this whole plot from a distance.
My first move was stealing home to Argos,
my second was winning Clytemnestra, my third
was setting this trap to kill your king.
He lies like an ugly dead fish in my net.
I killed him. I can die with honor.

CHORUS

You'll die. We are glad to give you the sole
honors you claim for plotting this murder
from a safe distance. The people will stone you to death.

AEGISTHUS

So, you'll rush on the deck and threaten
your captain! Go below, get back to your benches.
You are old. Don't count on my mercy.
I have chains and soldiers, excellent surgeons
for teaching old men good manners.

CHORUS

You'll teach us. You woman! You slept
out the war in Clytemnestra's bed.

AEGISTHUS

I'll whip you in chains through the streets of my city.
Do you see your king lies killed?

CHORUS

Clytemnestra killed him. You hid behind
her skirts. You are Clytemnestra's mistress.

AEGISTHUS

Oh, deceiving and decoying Agamemnon to my trap
was work for a woman. I did the thinking.
I had to hold myself in. If this beast
had seen me, he would have smelled his death.
You see me now. You'll see me and feel me
day and night. I have Clytemnestra.
I have Agamemnon's money. I am your tyrant.
I will be the wonder and terror of Greece.
You won't run loose like cornfed colts,
you won't grow fat at the feeding trough.

CHORUS

[*Drawing their swords*]

You have called yourself our tyrant, Aegisthus.
You will die like a tyrant. Do you see our swords?
We are ready to die, if you are.

AEGISTHUS

[*Motioning to his* GUARD]

My sword is ready. It's a good one.
Do you see it, old men?

[*Turns to* GUARD]

                 Move in, men.
Cut them down. They are sheep.

CLYTEMNESTRA

[*As* CLYTEMNESTRA *comes forward, both sides draw back and
gradually sheathe their swords*]

No, have mercy on them, my dearest.
We've done enough. We must rest from the harvest.
Go back to your homes, my friends, and live out
your lives in peace. You have done what you could;
we too have only done what we had to.
Oh let us do no more harm!
I have watched over this house like a mother.
A woman is speaking to you, try
to understand.

CHORUS

We believe you,
Clytemnestra. You have done what you could.

[*Pause. The* CHORUS *starts to go*]

We warn you Orestes will return from exile.
You must die by the hand of your son.

AEGISTHUS

An exile lives on empty hopes.
I know. I was one.

CLYTEMNESTRA

Forget their grumbling. They are old and weak,
my dearest. You and I have the power
to bring back obedience to this house.

ORESTES

Characters

ORESTES

PYLADES

CHORUS OF SLAVE WOMEN

ELECTRA

SERVANT (DOORKEEPER)

CLYTEMNESTRA

CILISSA

AEGISTHUS

FOLLOWER OF AEGISTHUS

SERVANTS

FURIES

ORESTES

[*Scene: a field outside the palace of Atreus. Black of early morning. Two men,* ORESTES *and* PYLADES, *move into the half light toward a grassy mound, the grave of Agamemnon*]

ORESTES

I am home. I walk the earth
of my own kingdom. All's familiar.
Just as was planned, just as I planned,
I've come to the mound of my Father's grave,
a shapeless sprawl, a dim green
in the darkness of my kingdom—not yet my kingdom.

[ORESTES *kneels at his father's grave, and places a knot of scarlet feathers on it*]

Ah my Father, I was in exile,
I could not save you, weep for you, or bury you.
Now I am a man. I am here.
I claim my rights, and here at your grave,
Agamemnon, I offer you
these locks of my hair, this blood-knot
of red feathers dipped in blood.
Blood of your blood, I ask for blood.

[*The* CHORUS OF SLAVE WOMEN *begins to enter indistinctly at the side of the stage. They carry urns of wine to pour on the grave of Agamemnon.* ELECTRA *follows them*]

PYLADES

Stand up Orestes. Let's stand back a little.
I see a line of black shadows.
They are marching on us. They are carrying something.

ORESTES

[*He stands*]

I see them, Pylades. They're only women,
who look like shadows because they are
in mourning and wear black veils.
They are slave women carrying urns
of wine to pour on Father's grave.
Some new disaster has struck our house.
These women wish to appease the dead king,
and supplicate the gods of the underworld.
Do you see that sorrowing woman coming last?
I know her. She is my Sister,
Electra. Oh Zeus, God of justice,
stand beside us and fight for our cause.
Help me revenge the murder of my Father.

PYLADES

Let's speak to your Sister.

ORESTES

No, wait.

I trust Electra, but I fear
my own flesh and blood here in Clytemnestra's city.
Let's take cover. We'll watch and learn.

[ORESTES *and* PYLADES *withdraw. The* CHORUS *comes forward to the grave. They group around* ELECTRA *and speak to her one by one*]

ONE

Let us rest, Electra. We are bleeding.
They have whipped us to work, and now they whip
us from their house, and force us to carry
their urns of supplication to the angry king.
My clothes have been torn from my body. They've made
me gash my cheeks with my own hands.

TWO

I am glad to leave the palace of Atreus,
but here by the grave of your Father, Princess,
I still hear his spirit smolder.
The woman had a dream. Agamemnon's ghost is stalking
through her inner bedroom. She asks us to wash
away the blood that was spilled on the ground.

THREE

Nothing will wash away this blood.
So much blood has fallen on our earth,
it is caked and hard and nothing drains off.
Disaster waits, the infection boils.
Some have fallen in their brightness. Others
will walk to their death in the cowardly night.

FOUR

All's one to us. The gods have destroyed
our cities and burned our fathers' houses.
They have led us here as slaves.
Our wills are twisted to the wills of our masters.
Right and wrong are one. We obey.
Electra, we weep for the wrong that killed your Father.

ELECTRA

Dear friends and my attendants, advise me. Let's speak
together, since we were sent here together
to pour libations at Agamemnon's grave.
How can I pour out my urn? What
can I say to my Father. Shall I say:
"A loving wife empties this loving
cup to her beloved husband"? That wife
is Clytemnestra! I am afraid
to speak such a lie. But what else can I say?
I know the customary formula for these prayers:
"Spirit, give the givers of these gifts
what they deserve." What *they* deserve
is blood for blood. Shall I say this?
No, I will stand and say nothing.
I'll throw out this wine like dirty water,
then turn my back on it, as if I'd emptied garbage.
I'll toss my jar out of sight and break it.

You must advise me and share my burden.
We have shared the savagery of this house—
I free, you as slaves. All slaves!
I too am a slave in my Father's house.
Ah friends, I stand here dishonored and helpless
as my Father, when this suppliant killed him.

CHORUS

Here by your Father's tomb, this sacred altar,
I beg you to pour out the wine. As you pour,
pray for his friends who are faithful.

ELECTRA

Who is faithful?

CHORUS

Yourself and those who hate Aegisthus.

ELECTRA

I'll pray for myself and you, my friends.
There's no one else.

CHORUS

Pray for your Brother, Orestes, who wanders in exile.

ELECTRA

I pray for my poor Brother's return.

CHORUS

Pray simply for a man to come. Pray
for a man to take the lives of those
who have taken a life.

ELECTRA

Can I do this? The gods curse
us for striking our own . . . They struck first, though . . .
Gods of the underworld, hear me!
Hear me, Oh earth! All things rise
from thee, great earth, and prevail for their little
lives, then sink again in thee.
Hear me, my Father! As I pour this wine
in atonement on your grave, I call you. Father,
pity me, pity your Son, Orestes.
How can we live or rule our house.

Wanderers and slaves, we were sold by our Mother.
With our heritage, she bought Aegisthus,
who helped her cut you down, my Father.
Agamemnon, I live as a slave in your house.
Orestes, your Son, the king of this land,
is banished from his great possessions.
But *they* are not banished, *they* are not slaves.
They live off the wealth of what you worked
to win. Oh may the gods bring
Orestes back to his own. I ask the earth,
all-conquering Justice and all the gods
to send us our avenger. Agamemnon,
I demand that your killers be killed as they killed!
For myself, I ask for a purer heart
than my Mother's and cleaner hands.

> [ELECTRA *pours her urn on the grave. The* CHORUS *pour their urns, and as they pour they chant*]

ONE

King Agamemnon, King of Argos,
we pour this red wine on your grave,
and pray that the blood of your killers may also
be poured out on the ground. Hear us,
Agamemnon! Listen with your dark heart.

TWO

We pray for the coming of the man of power.
He will come as a Scythian warlord,
his bow will be stretched tight in his hands,
he will spatter the tyrants with his arrows,
his sword will slash at close quarters.

ELECTRA

Father, the earth has drunk this wine
I have poured for those who are faithful.

[*She sees the blood-knot*]

What is this?

CHORUS

It's a knot of scarlet eagle feathers.
They are tied with human hair.

ELECTRA

These eagle feathers were dipped in blood.
They couldn't have come from our house.

CHORUS

We don't understand you. Who could have brought them?

ELECTRA

Someone who has sworn to avenge Agamemnon.
I think Orestes may have sent them.

CHORUS

Your Brother wouldn't dare return to Argos.

ELECTRA

Perhaps he wouldn't. But when I look at these
red feathers, it's as though someone
had slashed a sword across my heart.
It's as though my own blood stained them.
Perhaps my Mother . . . I have no Mother.
Ours hates her children. Maybe the mistress
of Aegisthus left this knot of eagle
feathers to tell me I must die.

Why does it lie on Agamemnon's grave?
Whoever left it wished to avenge
my Father's murder. I think Orestes . . .
The gods know. We pray to the gods,
and they spin us round in circles like sailors.
I wish these feathers had a voice.
A great tree will grow from this small seed.
Oh this confusion! My mind is groping.
What's this? Men are moving through the night.

ORESTES

Thank God, the night is passed. Pray
for the morning, Electra. Pray for success.

ELECTRA

Who are you? Why do you call me Electra?

ORESTES

No one has a truer right, Electra.

ELECTRA

Have you come from my Brother, Orestes?

ORESTES

I am even closer to you, Electra.

ELECTRA

No one is closer. My God . . . my Orestes!

ORESTES

Yes, we are speaking face to face.
Sister, you hardly believe me,
and yet you shuddered and knew I was near,
when you first saw the knot of feathers.

Do you see this hunter killing the wolf
and his bitch on this piece of tapestry?
You wove it with your own hands, and sent it
to me in my exile. Don't show your joy.
Those nearest wish to kill us.

ELECTRA

My dear Brother. I have wept
for you, prayed for you, hoped for you!
You are my Father, my Sister, my Mother.
May the gods have mercy on Agamemnon
and his ignorant hand that slaughtered Iphigenia.
As for my Mother . . . I have no Mother.
May her name die. You are my Brother,
my family, my blood . . . May
Almighty Zeus stand at our side!

ORESTES

Almighty Zeus, look down and guide us.
Orestes and Electra stand before you,
children without a father, and driven
from their house. We are fledglings of the eagle-
father, who was strangled in the coils of a snake.
Guide us! We were caught in a cage by the oppressor.
We could not bring food to our shelter. Oh Sky-god,
who will honor you with sacrifice,
if the young of the eagle are killed?

CHORUS

Speak more quietly, children. I fear
some traitor from love of gossip will warn
the tyrants. I wish I saw the body
of Aegisthus crackling on the pyre of pitch.

ORESTES

I'm not afraid. The Oracle of Apollo
has spoken. Apollo at Delphi has commanded
me to kill my Father's killers.
I must rush on the hunters with a lion's fury
and recover my city. No money
will pay their price. If I falter
and disobey this command, I shall die.
Doom shall rise from the earth. The dead
shall curse the coward. Ulcers and scabs
will cover my body and riddle its tissue.
White hairs will wriggle from my flesh.
I shall whiten with leprosy.
My Father's Furies—their eyes move
and see clearly in the dark, they will watch me,
shake me, tear me, and drive me mad!
Broken by the night's blind terrors,
I'll hide from the day, or cower under
the tyrant's bronze-slugged whip.
I will lose my city. No one will let
me drink wine from the common cup,
or give me bread. No house for shelter!
Agamemnon's wrath
will drive me back from the shrines of the gods.
I shall die sick and wasted,
the outcast, the coward.

This is what the gods promise me.
I fear them, I obey them.
If I should escape their curse, I would

be cursed by men. I am driven by my love
for my Father. I will not let my possessions
slip from my hand. Oh Argos, Argos,
I will not let our people, the destroyers
of Troy and Hector, serve as slaves here
under two women. Aegisthus
is a woman. If he is a man,
he must show me.

CHORUS

Zeus, almighty Zeus,
let the wheel of vengeance turn
full circle on the killers.
Hatred for hatred, blood
for blood, and life for life.
A man must kill now to live.

ORESTES

Father, Oh King of Argos,
I stand in a far place;
nothing I can say or do
will reach you, huddled in the dark.
Nothing will bring you light,
yet I mourn for our great house.

CHORUS

My Child, the fire that burns
and tears with its teeth at the dead man
never wears away
his will for vengeance. A man
dies, he is buried. Light
finds the guilty and kills him.

ELECTRA

Hear me, Father, hear me.
Two children stand at your grave.
Your grave is our only house.
We give you the tears of our sorrow,
but what good
is grief at the grave?

CHORUS

The gods, if they wish, can change
our wailing to shouts of triumph.
Orestes will regain his house.

ORESTES

Ah my Father, if you had died
at Troy, cut down by its spearmen,
you would have left great
glory to our house.
Men would have honored your Son;
I might have walked the streets of Argos.

CHORUS

You should have died fighting,
Agamemnon. In the underworld,
you would have been honored by the heroes
who died in battle, by those
who loved you, King of Kings.
On the earth, you ruled men, whose hands
held powers of life and death.

ELECTRA

No, my Father, you should not
have died at Troy, and lie

now with the nameless thousands
of your soldiers on the banks of the Scamander.
Your murderers should have been killed
at home, as you were, by those they loved.

CHORUS

Child, Child, you are dreaming.
North, north of the north wind!
This cannot be. But listen,
hell groans with you. The hands of those
who rule the earth are unclean.
Power grows on the side of the children.

ORESTES

The ground at my feet trembles.
Zeus, Zeus of the underworld,
rise like an earthquake and shake off
the crust of this earth. Strike
the hard heart and subtle hand.
Destruction will fall on the parents.

CHORUS

I claim the right to dance
the death-dance over the beheaded
tyrant and his fallen wife.
Why should I try to stifle
the black wind of loathing
and disgust that blows through my heart?

ELECTRA

May Zeus smash the brains
of the killers with his fist. Kill, kill!

Grind their skulls to powder!
These people must believe that wrong
has been done. Hear me, Oh earth!
Hear me, you terrors of darkness!

CHORUS

It's the law when once the red drops
have been spilled on the ground, they cry
out for fresh blood.

ORESTES

Assembled powers of darkness, hear
the curse of my Father. The last
of the sons of Atreus is lost.
He is cast from the sunlight of Argos.
Father, where shall I turn?

CHORUS

My heart falters when I hear
you cry out in fear,
my King, but now my fury
exalts me. I am lifted on the wings
of hope. My eyes are brightness.

ELECTRA

What shall I say that will strike
deeper than my Mother's words?
Let her fawn for favors, if she likes.
I am the true daughter of the wolf,
as bloody as the wolf that bore me.

CHORUS

She struck again and again
without stopping, now upward, now downward.
Fists like drifting hail
hammering and hammering on my head.
I was gashed like a Scythian mourner.

ELECTRA

Oh cruel, cruel wife,
she stopped at nothing. The people
of Argos were banished from the funeral.
His subjects forgot him. Agamemnon,
you were buried without tears.

ORESTES

Why do you say more of my dishonor?
Surely my Mother shall pay
for the degradation of Agamemnon.
By the immortals, by my hands! . . . I want
to take her life and die.

CHORUS

Listen, Orestes, I will tell you
something you have no strength to bear.
When Clytemnestra buried Agamemnon,
she cut off his feet and hands,
and hung them under his armpits.

ELECTRA

Ah Brother, you have heard
how our Father was mutilated.

I was dishonored, I was pushed aside.
I was kenneled in a dark corner,
and chained like a mad dog.

CHORUS

With a burning yet quiet heart,
you will remember all you have heard.
Things are as they are, Orestes.
Yours now the future. Be hard,
give no ground, and kill.

[*The* CHORUS *moves away slightly from* ORESTES *and* ELECTRA, *who continue speaking in alternating ritualistic voices. As they speak, they kneel at Agamemnon's grave*]

ORESTES

Father, I call to you.
Stand by those you love.

ELECTRA

Father, I weep for you.
Death cannot weaken my love.

ORESTES

Sword shall break on sword.
Right shall clash with right.

ELECTRA

Look on us and be just, Oh gods,
and may the good prevail.

ORESTES

Father, you did not die as a king.
Give me back the rule of my house.

ELECTRA

Give me just this, Oh my Father:
Let me kill Aegisthus and live.

ORESTES

Think of the bath, Agamemnon.
There you died in your blood.

ELECTRA

Think of the net, my Father.
You couldn't struggle when you died.

ORESTES

Agamemnon, you were caught in the net
and hacked to death like a wolf.

ELECTRA

Hear one more cry from me, my Father.
This is my last. Your children kneel
as suppliants at your tomb. Pity us.
Do not blot out the seed of your house.
When you died, you did not entirely die.
Your children are the breath of your salvation.
Like corks we buoy up the knotted meshes
of the drenched net. Your house will not drown.
Hear us, hear us. Father, save
yourself by hearing my supplication.

[CHORUS *speaking to each other, somewhat detached and
bewildered*]

CHORUS

My heart sinks inside me, when I hear
Electra pray. We have waited long

for the day of vengeance. The children call for it.
What will happen will happen.

SECOND VOICE

Do not blame Electra for the length
of her prayers. She is standing by her Brother.
She weeps for the unwept body of Agamemnon.
What will happen is murder.

[ORESTES *leaves* ELECTRA *and turns to the* CHORUS]

ORESTES

Tell me this. Agamemnon was killed
without feeling. Why does Clytemnestra
now order these libations for the dead?
Years late, she offers this insulting reparation
for a crime that has no price. Let
her pour out all her possessions:
Nothing can atone for one act of murder.
Everybody knows this trifling is useless.

CHORUS

Son of Agamemnon, my Child,
I know the reason. I was there. Your Mother,
the godless Clytemnestra, had a dream.
She dreamed she gave birth to a snake.
She swaddled it, as if it were her child,
and gave her breast to suck,
and the snake sucked out milk and blood,
and wounded her breast. Then she woke screaming.
Torches were lit all over the house.
She sent these offerings to appease
the drifting terrors of the black night.

ORESTES

This all hangs together. I will succeed.

Let no one dispute my interpretation.
Out of my Mother's womb, a snake
crawled to the light of day. She wrapped
the hideous creature in soft clothes,
and gave it her soft breast to suck.
The snake sucked blood and milk.
I too crawled from the same place.
I was wrapped, was suckled. My Mother's
life blood shall give me life.

CHORUS

No one shall dispute your interpretation.
Orestes, tell us what to do.
We shall act or not act, as you wish.

ORESTES

Attendants on my Sister, your instructions are simple.
Stand and watch. Electra shall go
inside the palace and quiet the fear there.
Pylades and I shall knock on the palace doors.
Who'll know me? Years have gone. I am dressed
as a Phocian merchant. How can the hard
Mother recognize the Son
she exiled and would never look at?
Even Electra thought I was a stranger.
Tell Clytemnestra we are emissaries
from a far country.
I will tell her Orestes is dead.
Go, my Sister. Let your ladies follow.
Your hand, Pylades. We are ready to kill.

PYLADES

My King the sun is rising. I obey.

[ELECTRA *leaves.* PYLADES *and* ORESTES *stand a minute then also leave. Stage darkens.* CHORUS *remains*]

FIRST VOICE

The dumb earth breeds
innumerable beasts, the sea's
arms seethe with monsters.
Torches stand like spears on the skyline.
Remember the wrath in the whirlwind.

SECOND VOICE

Who'll tell the horrible passions
of women, coupling and cramming
into the dark embrace
of marriage, they cripple the brute
beast and mortal man.

THIRD VOICE

The men of Lemnos were murdered
by their beloved wives and daughters.
Althea, the daughter of Thestius,
maimed her own son. His life
was shorter than the firebrand she lit at his birth.

FOURTH VOICE

Scylla adored the heavy
gold necklace of Minos.
For this she killed her Father.
She cut the immortal lovelock
of Nisus, but Hermes killed her.

THIRD VOICE

I welcome the quiet hearthlog.

FOURTH VOICE

I welcome the sleeping woman.

FIRST VOICE

The gods bring death to those they loathe.

SECOND VOICE

A sword shall cut through the woman's lungs.

FIRST VOICE

A son shall wash away
this bloodstain in the woman's blood.

[*Right of the stage lights up and shows the entrance of the palace of Atreus.* ORESTES *is knocking loudly on the door*]

ORESTES

You inside there! Does anyone hear me knocking?
I'll try again. Is anyone home.
Nobody! I'll try a third time. Hey there,
open up! Open the doors of the house.
Does Aegisthus bar his door to guests?

SERVANT   [*Opening the door*]

Easy, you'll knock the house down.
You can't be from Argos. Where do you come from?

ORESTES

Announce me to the master of the house, Man!
I have news for him. Hurry,
it's noon, the sun loiters in mid-sky,
but night's dark chariot is rushing on.

It's the hour for the wayfarer to drop anchor
in some place where all travelers have rest.
Have someone in authority come to us—
the lady of the house, perhaps, or better,
the lord, for a man takes courage
and will speak simply and clearly to another man.

CLYTEMNESTRA

[*She comes from the palace, still young but visibly older and
more tired than in the last play*]

Guests, tell me what you want,
and it shall be yours. We have all
the comforts that go with a great house:
hot baths, couches that ease away
fatigue, gentle hands and eyes.
But if you come on some matter of state,
that's business for men, and men will attend you.

ORESTES

I am a stranger from Daulis out of Phocis.
As I was journeying to Argos, lugging my merchandise
on my back, I met a stranger. He said,
"I am Strophius, the Phocian. Where are you going?"
"To Argos," I answered. He said, "Friend,
since you are going to Argos on your own
business, I beg you to tell Orestes'
parents he is dead. Be sure you tell
the right people. They will decide
if they want his ashes brought home,
or buried in Phocis, forever in exile.
The young man has been honorably mourned,
a bronze urn holds his ashes."

All this was told me by Strophius, the Phocian.
I know no more. I wonder if I am
talking now to someone in authority.
I think the young man's Father should be told.

CLYTEMNESTRA

Ah me, the house of Atreus is thundering
to ruin on our heads. We have hidden
our precious things, but the arch-enemy
has seen from far and shot us down.
I've lost every thing I ever loved.
I believed Orestes was safely exiled
from this swamp of destruction. He wasn't.
Far, far from Argos, he has died.
Our bright star of hope is ashes.

ORESTES

I wish I could have brought good news,
and earned the kind reception this house
always gives a stranger from a far country.
Nothing is more lovely than the feeling
between guest and host. But I gave my word.
You look sorrowful. I must tell you the truth.

CLYTEMNESTRA

Stranger, you shall be received worthily.
You are no less our friend for your news.
If you hadn't, someone else would have told us.
But now it's the hour when the foot-weary traveler
should pause and receive the rest he deserves.
Come, my servants, and escort this merchant
and his companion to the men's halls of the palace.

I entrust the honor of our house to you.
While you are resting, Friend, I'll talk to the king.

[CLYTEMNESTRA *goes into the palace.* ORESTES *and* PYLADES
follow, led by the servants through another door]

CHORUS

FIRST VOICE

Dear Handmaidens of the house,
I wish our weak words were swords
to help Orestes in his hour of trial.

SECOND VOICE   [*Kneeling*]

Dear Earth, Queen Earth,
you lie like a garment on the king of ships.
Hear us and help our king in his danger.

THIRD VOICE

Now Strategy and Hermes, the subtle killer,
join hands and point to the pit.
Now the sword's edge is razor-sharp.

FIRST VOICE

I think the Stranger is beginning his bloody work.
Look, Orestes' old nurse is coming
in tears. Why are you weeping, Cilissa?

CILISSA

The woman who calls herself our mistress
has ordered me to hurry and call Aegisthus
for the stranger. She said he will speak simply
and clearly to Aegisthus, as man to man.
Before the slaves, Clytemnestra's eyes
were half smiling and half scowling, but she could not

hide her happiness at what she had heard.
What she heard was the death of our house.
But the Tyrant, Aegisthus, will be happy enough.
That woman will show his feelings simply
and clearly like a man. Ah poor Cilissa!
how many years I have suffered the pollution
and anguish of this house: murder, exile,
and usurpation! My heart aches
in my breast, but never before as now.
Orestes, my Darling, you are dead!
I took you from your Mother's arms, nursed you,
and wore away my life in your care.
Often you screamed at night and woke me,
for a child is an animal, isn't it?
It has no speech to tell us it is hungry
or thirsty or wants to make water.
A child's belly is a law to itself.
I had prophetic sight, but often I erred.
Then I was both a nurse and a laundress.
King Agamemnon could find no one else
to mother his son! Orestes is dead.
Our King is dead, and now I must run
and call Aegisthus, the Squatter in this house.
He will be glad to hear the news.

CHORUS

Did Clytemnestra say Aegisthus would come
back armed?

CILISSA

What do you mean? I said . . .

CHORUS

Will Aegisthus come with his bodyguard?

CILISSA

She said for him to come in state with his cutthroats.

CHORUS

Cilissa, if you despise the tyrant,
rush in on him, and tell
him to come quickly and speak to the stranger
alone, as man to man.
The stranger will make the crooked sentence straight.

CILISSA

Why are you rejoicing? Orestes is dead.

CHORUS

You say so, but perhaps Zeus will change
evil to good.

CILISSA

No good, no good!
Orestes the hope of our house is gone!

CHORUS

Only a false prophet would say this.

CILISSA

You know something you haven't told me.

CHORUS

Go, Cilissa, do as you are told.
The gods' affairs are the gods' affairs.

CILISSA

Slaves, I will go and do as you
have told me; may the good prevail.

[CILISSA *returns to the palace*]

FIRST VOICE

Father of the gods on Olympus,
look down from your high places, and help
the man who works hard.
He will bring restraint to his violence,
and order to the house of Atreus.

SECOND VOICE

Zeus, Zeus, help
the stranger who has entered this house,
and already spars for his death-lock
with those who hate. Orestes will reward
you three times over, Oh Zeus!

THIRD VOICE

Look at the colt of the King
of Kings. He has taken on
the heavy harness of suffering.
Let him run straight in the bridle.
Let him reach the widening goal.

SECOND VOICE

Long, long, the head
of this house has lain crushed
under a helmet of blackness.
Let the eyes be quick again.
Let them look the sun in the face.

FIRST VOICE

Go, Stranger, and when death
cries, 'Child,' answer,
'Father, Father, I have come.'
He will take on the innocence of murder,
and kill the man of blood.

[AEGISTHUS *enters. He has an air of hurried, bossy querulousness, that mars his kingly façade*]

AEGISTHUS

You speak of blood. We do not come
unsummoned. Orestes' old nurse
speaks of blood in Phocis. Strangers
from Phocis told her of Orestes' death.
This news brings us no joy. Our Kingdom
still totters under its old infection of blood.
But is this news or a rumor? We know well
how the timidity and hysterias of women
fill the air with ridiculous omens.
They are empty. Speak to me, Women. Is
there any sense in this stranger's story?

CHORUS

We heard the rumor, but we are women,
as you say, easily mistaken, more
easily alarmed. Go inside
and meet the stranger who'll answer your queries
simply and clearly, as man to man.

AEGISTHUS

We will examine and test the stranger
with care. What we desire is an eyewitness,

someone who has actually seen Orestes
die, not some exotic alarmist.
I am Aegisthus, the far-sighted.
No one has ever blinded the eye of my mind.

[AEGISTHUS *returns to the palace by another door*]

FIRST VOICE

Zeus, Zeus, give
me words for my prayer. My will
is good, but I have no words.

SECOND VOICE

Listen, the sword slides
gently from the scabbard. Its edge
is freedom, but who will die?

THIRD VOICE

Light rushes into the house
of Atreus. Dominion crashes
to its long-expected ruin.

SECOND VOICE

Stand ready, the sword is sunlight
and freedom. The Son will possess
all the bright gold of the Father.

FIRST VOICE

Poor Son, poor Wayfarer, he must wrestle
with two of his own blood, not one.
He is doomed to throw them both.

AEGISTHUS   [*From inside*]

I've been stabbed. Help me. I've been killed.

FIRST VOICE

Listen, the voice of Agamemnon! The wheel
has gone full circle, but who has died?

SECOND VOICE

Let us stand aside. What had
to be done was done without our help.

FOLLOWER OF AEGISTHUS

[Enters distractedly from a side door]

What's done is done. Cry sorrow, sorrow,
sorrow, they've killed my king. Aegisthus
is dead. Open the palace gates.
Open the doors to the women's apartments.
Hurry, hurry, a strong arm
is needed, but no strength in the world will rouse
Aegisthus. He's dead. What's done is done.
Speak, Women! Help me! Am I talking
to the deaf and dumb? Go call Clytemnestra.
Where is she? What is the Queen doing?
Her soft neck is on the axe's edge.
The ripe fruit is ready to fall.

CLYTEMNESTRA

What's this? Why are you shouting like a madman
in my house?

FOLLOWER

The dead are killing the living.

CLYTEMNESTRA

Yes, yes, you speak in tiresome riddles,
but I catch your meaning. The stranger is stealing

my own stealth and stratagems to kill us.
You say my throat is on the axe's edge.
Bring me an axe. Quick, quick!
We'll see whose throat? Everybody knows
I can kill a man.

   [*Exit* FOLLOWER]

        We'll see. I'm lost,
but not so entirely lost that I'll die
without killing my killer, no matter who.

   [*Enter* ORESTES *and* PYLADES]

   ORESTES

You're next. The man inside the women's
apartments has given up.

   CLYTEMNESTRA

        Ah Aegisthus!
Come and stand beside me, my Beloved,
you have made the fire shine at my hearth.

   ORESTES

You loved him. He'll never stand again.
You shall fear no unfaithfulness, when you lie
together in death, as you lay in life.

   CLYTEMNESTRA

Child, I know you. Stand back from me. Here
you dreamed and played. Here are the breasts
you sucked with your soft gums and grew strong.

   ORESTES

What shall I do, Pylades? Dare I
murder the Wife of my Father, my own Mother?

PYLADES

Kill the killer of Agamemnon. Apollo
has spoken. The gods guide you. Will
you be hateful to the gods, as well as to man?

ORESTES

I obey, Pylades. My flesh and blood
have betrayed me, I will not betray the gods,
The Furies of my Father . . .

                                    Come with me, Clytemnestra . . .
No, I'll not name you. I intend to kill you
over the body of Aegisthus. Once
you thought he was greater than my Father. Die then,
sleep soundly on top of the man you love.
You destroyed the man you should have loved.

CLYTEMNESTRA

I brought you up, when you were little, Orestes.
I wish to grow old with you.

ORESTES

You killed my Father, now you wish
to grow old in the house of your son. You have none.

CLYTEMNESTRA

I had a loved daughter, Iphigenia.
Agamemnon took her from me and butchered her.
These deaths were determined by the gods, Orestes.

ORESTES

Say your own death is determined by the gods.
You are no mother. When you bore me, you sold me
in exile.

CLYTEMNESTRA

I sent you to friends for safety,
I never sold you.

ORESTES

For whose safety? You had your price.

CLYTEMNESTRA

What price?

ORESTES

Argos and something I will not name
that waits for you in the women's apartments.

CLYTEMNESTRA

Name Cassandra and your Father's other pleasures.

ORESTES

He saved Argos, while your pleasure sat at home.

CLYTEMNESTRA

Child, you do not know what an abandoned wife suffers.

ORESTES

Agamemnon faced death for his people and Argos.

CLYTEMNESTRA

Ah my Child, you will kill your Mother. Take care,
my curse will tear you and drag you to the ground like a dog.
I feel as if I were talking to a tomb.

ORESTES

I shall escape the curse of my Father.
It's you who have chosen to kill yourself.

CLYTEMNESTRA

Ah Child, you are the snake I bore and suckled.

ORESTES

I know your dream. Your dream is true.
Come, you must die for the man who died.

[ORESTES *leads* CLYTEMNESTRA *into the palace*]

FIRST VOICE

I must grieve even for this terrible
bride and bridegroom. They had their splendor,
but let us hail Orestes, who cut the blood-chain.
The eye of our house has not fallen in blindness.

SECOND VOICE

I too hail Orestes, he has purified
the house of Atreus of its two tyrants,
who wasted its beauty. They coiled like two
poisonous snakes on its crimson tapestries.

THIRD VOICE

A man came back. His work was hard
and furtive, but the gods were our helpers—Zeus,
Hermes and Athena! Listen, the wind
of the gods is the breath of death on the defiler.

SECOND VOICE

Apollo screamed from Parnassus. His will
was justice and murder. He gave us strength
never to give in to the wicked. Once more
we can worship the majesty and power of the sky.

FIRST VOICE

Time makes all things right perhaps.
Orestes has washed the blood from his house.
He has cast out its age-old furies.
The dice have fallen right.

> [*The palace doors are thrown open. Aegisthus' body is
> brought in, then Clytemnestra's is thrown on top of it.* ORESTES
> *stands a little in front of them.* PYLADES *holds up the noosed
> and weighted robe that Agamemnon was killed in. Somehow
> the sight of the robe seems to madden* ORESTES]

ORESTES

Attendants on my Sister, look at them.
They are both here. Here are the two tyrants,
who killed my Father and plundered his house.
They lived their season, enjoyed their two
thrones, all the loftiness of the state.
They are still lovers. They said nothing lightly,
when they took counsel together, and swore
they'd kill my Father and die together.
They've died together. They've kept their oath.

Look, I have the robe and net
they contrived for my Father. This part entangled
his hands. Here's the clog for his feet.
Spread it out. Stand round
in a circle. Here's the net that caught a man.
My Father shall see it. No, more than my Father . . .
the all-seeing Father, the sun,
shall look down on my Mother's robe,
and bear me witness on my day of trial.

It was right I achieved her death.
I speak of my Mother. I pass over
Aegisthus. He died as all adulterers
must die by law. The laws take
care of him, but I speak of my Mother.
She thought up this robe for my Father.
Once she carried his children, and seemed to love them.
Soon they were hated. What shall I call
this daring ruler? An asp? a watersnake?
Even before it was touched, this brutal
coil of scales rotted our hands.

What shall I call this robe. Is it a trap?
a winding sheet? a bath-curtain
for a dead man? A robber might invent
and own a thing like this. Some coward who wouldn't
even risk his safety for the money he'd set
his heart on!

May this kind of wife never live with me.
I'd rather die childless!

CHORUS

They lie like lovers. Ah Clytemnestra,
a dishonorable death has ended your daring
dishonorable life. You leave a son.
He is your killer, your heir. His torture increases.

ORESTES

She did it. She did it. Look, my proof
is this great, weighted robe. Here,
here's where she stained Aegisthus' sword.

Here! Here! She dug in, she dipped it
again and again. Look how time
and caking blood have conspired to spoil
this kingly garment. I shall praise the King.
His death is paid for. I trample on the web
that killed him.

> [ORESTES *stumbles and becomes partially entangled in the robe*]

Not yet, not yet, I am entangled
in my kingship. I grieve for what I have done.
I have triumphed, my triumph is stained.
No pride, no pride!

CHORUS

Alas, no mortal man shall run
unwounded to the goal. Orestes is stained
with his own blood. His torture increases.

ORESTES

I grieve for what I have done. I see
no end. I am a charioteer colliding
with another. Beaten from the track, I wander
far from my course. Friends, my mind
and senses crash together. Listen!
I feel my heart pounding like a boxer's
weighted fist on my ribs. Always
the beat is rising, as if I led the singers
in the dance of anger through Argos to their deaths.
No, wait! My mind is still whole. I declare
publicly: I was right to kill my Mother.
Agamemnon's blood was on her hands.

The gods' disgust at her guided my hand.
No, it was no light thing or trivial
magic that led me. Apollo spoke.
He promised if I did as I did, I wouldn't suffer.
And yet I suffer. There's no evasion.
No arrow can hit the height of my pain.
Look, I am picking up the green branch
and garland of supplication. With such weapons,
I shall go to the stone and shrine
of my patron, Apollo. I will go to the famous
fire that never dies to wash
my own blood from my hands. It's mine, mine, so
all men in the future shall remember how
I found good in evil and evil in good.
Once more I shall go out from Argos as an outcast.
I am Agamemnon's loyal son and Clytemnestra's killer.

CHORUS

Do not speak such evil against yourself,
my King. You are the liberator of Argos.
Say simply: what was done
was well done. Say, "I
have lopped off the heads of two snakes."

[*Clytemnestra's* FURIES *appear.* ORESTES *points to them. No
one else sees them*]

ORESTES

No, no, Attendants on Electra,
look closely. There are other
women in this house now. They too wear black,
but they are wreathed with snakes. They draw

their old swords and point to Orestes.
I cannot stay here.

CHORUS

You see nothing, Nothing blackens
your eyes. You are dear to the gods and your Father.
Do not give in to your fears, Orestes.

ORESTES

Black, black! What's here is here.
I see the truth. I see the Furies.
These are the bloodhounds of my Mother's curse.
Don't you see them. If I moved a little,
and stretched out my hand, I could touch them.

CHORUS

No, Orestes, you only see
the blood on your hands, your righteous blood.
Too much Justice has shaken your eyesight and courage.

ORESTES

Apollo, Apollo, help me! They move
nearer, more and more of them!
Each hand is pointing me down. Help me, Women!

CHORUS

Call on Apollo, the far-sighted,
my King. We see nothing. Soon
you will see nothing, only this liberated
kingdom and your Mother's blood.

ORESTES
You don't see them, but I do.

[ORESTES *staggers off the stage followed by the* FURIES]

THE FURIES

Characters

PYTHIAN PRIESTESS

ORESTES

FURIES (CHORUS OF WOMEN)

APOLLO

GHOST OF CLYTEMNESTRA

ATHENA

HERMES

JURORS

HERALD

THE FURIES

[*The first part of the play takes place in Delphi before the shrine of the Pythian Apollo. The rest of the play is at Athens on the Acropolis before Athena's temple*]

[*Enter alone, the* PYTHIAN PRIESTESS]

PRIESTESS

I must give first place in my prayers to the Earth,
before all the gods, she was a prophetess.
Next I honor the sons of Hephaestus,
workers in metal and builders of roads,
who changed the wilderness to farm and city.
With Hephaestus I honor Dionysus
whose drunken worshippers hunted
King Pentheus to his death like a hare.
I am seated on my throne. If any Greeks are here,
let them draw lots to enter, as is the custom.
I can only prophesy what the god directs.

[*She enters the shrine and suddenly reappears*]

Things terrible to tell or see with my eyes
drive me back from the house of Apollo.
I have no strength, I cannot stand on my feet—
I run on my hands. A frightened old woman
is nothing . . . less than a child.
I was on my way to the altar hung with wreaths,

when I saw a man standing at the centerstone;
the defilement of a god was on him.
He was a suppliant, yet blood dripped from his hands.
He had just drawn his sword and held an olive branch
wrapped ritualistically in white wool.
The fleece shone. This much I can say clearly,
but then I saw a fearful troop of women.
They were in front of the man.
They lay sleeping on chairs by the altar.
Women? I would call them gorgons,
but they were different. In a painting once I saw
harpies tear the food from Phineas' hands. These women
had no wings, they were pure black.
When they snored, their breath made me fall backward.
Their eyes oozed, their dress was obscene
for the house of the god . . . even in a private house.
I have never seen such women, nor know
what land could safely claim them.

What happens from now on must be left to Apollo;
he heals by divination, clarifies the darkest omen—
he purifies the house of his servant.

> [*The doors of the temple open and show* ORESTES *and the
> sleeping* FURIES. APOLLO *and* HERMES *are beside him*]

APOLLO

I will not give you up. Until the end of your suffering,
I will protect you. Though far from you, I will be near.
I will have no mercy on your enemies, these ancient maidens.
They are like children gone gray with age;
see how easily I have trapped them in sleep—

Neither god nor man nor animal will come near them.
They are born because of our evil. They prosper
mostly in the darkness below the earth—
yet more feared than hated. In spite of my help,
you must run from them never taking breath.
They will follow your steps across winter fields,
when your driven feet will clumsily pound the earth.
You'll cross the sea too, see for an instant
marble harbors encircled by their safe bays.
Do not rush stupidly like a herd of stampeding sheep,
it is your own life you are guarding.
I will not fail you, I will lead you to Athena's city.
Kneel there, and take her ancient image in your arms.
You will find just judges in that place.
Their words will mysteriously absolve you,
and you will go free in your innocence.
For it was I who made you kill your mother.

ORESTES

King Apollo, you understand how easily we do wrong;
may you also pardon the loyalty of a servant—
none doubts your power to do good, if you wish.

APOLLO

You must not distrust me out of fear.

[*Turning to* HERMES]

Hermes, my dear brother, watch over Orestes;
you are the god of guidance, and he is my servant.
Shepherd him on his long criminal journey
to its fortunate end.
An outlaw has rights the gods must respect.

[APOLLO *leaves, then* HERMES *leading* ORESTES. *The ghost of*
CLYTEMNESTRA *enters*]

CLYTEMNESTRA

How can you still be sleeping?
You are no use to me dead. Wake up—
since you have neglected me, I wander
ashamed and abandoned among the other dead.
They abuse me unceasingly because I killed my husband;
none protests
the blow of my own son. He killed me.
The wound is under my heart . . . from my son's sword.
Look . . . though in daylight you cannot see
insubstantial things; yet in your dream,
the mind has eyes to see my slaughtered spirit.
How often I have poured libations to you—
soothing, sobering . . . without wine
to muddle your dogged heads.
I served them to you at midnight,
when no other god is banqueted.
Orestes has trampled these gifts underfoot;
he leaps lightly as a fawn from your unattended snare.
He has escaped, he is gone—
how he despises you. Ah Furies,
invincible powers of the depths,
listen to me and understand.
It is my life I entreat you for . . . my once life.
Clytemnestra rouses you from your dream.

[FURIES *blubber and growl in their sleep*]

You complain of work, but your prey has escaped.

My son has abler friends than mine;
they save him while you sleep.

[FURIES *mutter reproachfully*]

Why aren't you awake yet? Can't you feel guilt?
He is gone,
Orestes who killed his mother is gone.

[FURIES *make excited cries*]

Are you still whining and barking?
Wake up, stand up;
Evil is your province, it mourns your absence.

[*Increasing cries from the* FURIES]

Ah poor she-dragons, sleep and exhaustion
have drained the sources of your anger.

FURIES

Catch him, catch him, catch him, catch him, catch him.

CLYTEMNESTRA

In dreams you hunt your prey, barking and baying,
as if your hunger would never rest,
yet you do nothing. Are you so corrupted and conquered
by weariness that you can only sleep,
you forget my pain. Rise,
you must torment him with just accusations,
the cruel words of a quick conscience.
Breathe a mist of blood in his face from your throats and bellies.
Dry his hopes, hunt him to death.

[CLYTEMNESTRA *leaves. The* FURIES *begin to waken*]

FURIES ONE, TWO AND THREE [WOMEN]

FURY 1

Wake up . . . or are you awake?
Then wake our sister as I woke you.

FURY 2

Great wrong has been done me.
We have endured unendurable sufferings,
and all for nothing, because we fell asleep.
The hunted beast has broken from our trap.

[APOLLO *enters*]*

FURY 3

[*Turns to* APOLLO]

You are young and we are old.
Why have you ridden us down and stolen our captive?
He is an outlaw who killed his mother;
you too are an outlaw.

FURY 2

Even in my dreams, my reproach strikes me
like the cutting whip of a charioteer
or my executioner.
The weight of my guilt cannot be lifted.

FURY 3

Such are the workers of the younger gods—
your power is without conditions,
your throne runs with blood,
blood at the head, blood at the feet.
The center of the earth is rock.

---

* [I have added the stage directions marked with an asterisk. F.B.]

FURY 2

Though a god, you have dishonored your own shrine,
and set man's wishes against the ways of the gods,
and ruined the traditional distributions of power.

FURY 3

Though you have wounded us,
we shall not let this man escape.

FURY 1

From his own blood, another murderer
will come and take his life.

APOLLO

You have spoken. Get up and leave my house.

FURY 1

My lord Apollo, it is your turn to listen to us.
You are the principal in this crime,
Orestes' guilt is yours.

APOLLO

Go on speaking until I understand.

FURY 1

You ordered the outlaw to kill his mother.

APOLLO

Only to avenge his father.

FURY 1

Then you gave the murderer refuge in this house.

APOLLO

It's not for you to come near my shrine.

FURY 1

We have our duty,
it is to do what we have done.

APOLLO

What is this glorious and noble duty?

FURY 1

To avenge Clytemnestra . . . his mother he killed.

APOLLO

That woman killed her husband.

FURY 1

A husband is not a blood-relation like a son.

APOLLO

All marriage then, even that of Zeus and Hera,
comes to nothing.
Aphrodite herself becomes a fugitive,
though the sweetest thing in life is hers,
the marriage-bed allotted to man and woman,
greater than all oaths and revered by nature.
With what justice do you serve Clytemnestra
like slaves, and manhunt for her son?

FURY 1

Nothing will make me let that man go free.

APOLLO

Go after him then, and give yourselves more troubles.

FURY 1

Nothing will ever make me let that man escape.

APOLLO

Get out then quickly, or you will feel
the hiss and bite of the flying snake
sent from the twisted golden thong that strings my bow.
My house is no shelter for you. Go
where heads are cut off and eyes are gouged,
where young boys in all their glory are desexed,
where justice is mutilation and stoning and groans
of people in torture spiked through their spines
and stuck on walls. Go out, you herd of goats . . .
without a shepherd, since no god dare help you.

[*The* FURIES *exit.* APOLLO *exits*]*

[*The scene changes to Athens—the Acropolis, before the
temple of Athena*]*

[*Enter* ORESTES, *followed by the* FURIES]*

ORESTES

Lady, Athena, look at me. Apollo's will
has brought me to you.
I have been driven by cruel tormenters.
I have passed through many lands and cities.
I crossed the wild seas in my helplessness.
Suffering has blunted and worn away my guilt,
as Apollo wished. Judge me fairly, Goddess;
my hands that clasp your holy image
no longer run with a mother's blood.

FURY 1

How that blood still sticks to him.
Though it cannot speak, it calls on us to hurry.
We've followed him for many months like dogs;
until our breath was gone.

Without wings, we have crossed the seas.
We have caught the scent of the wounded hare now.
Look, he crouches and clutches the image of Athena.
It's nothing for him to cling to.

FURY 2

This smell of blood is sweet and comforting;
her blood flows over the place he stands on.
Nothing will wipe it away.
His hands cannot be clean,
until his lifeblood has joined his mother's.
Drop by drop, we will suck it from him.
It's a drink the gods and mortals turn from,
but I am not frightened.

FURY 3

Orestes,
we will drag you downward to the dark world.
Men who have killed those close to them
are punished there.
Look for justice there not here.

ORESTES

Since my misfortune, I must have entered
a thousand asylums and temples of absolution—
in some I had to speak, in others be silent.
I know I must stand firm here, and later
defend my life; for so Apollo plans.
I see the stain on my hands grows dim
and wears away. I can hardly see it.
When will I no longer suffer my mother's curse?
When her blood was fresh on me,

I was purified by slaughtered swine
in Apollo's temple. Since then I cannot say
how often I have stood and told men
the story of her death. No one condemned me.
Time forgets, with a clear conscience.
I now call to Athena, the deity of this shrine.
My kingdom of Argos will love and serve you.
Lady, hear me wherever you are—
in one of your sacred hiding places,
or shadowing the scorching deserts of Libya,
or moving in arms like a soldier on the field of Phlegra.
O irresistible supporter of your friends,
listen to me. A god can hear from afar;
Athena come to me. My enemies have tracked me down.

FURY 1

You must know you are lost—
neither Athena's forbearance
nor the crooked mind of Apollo,
your fellow-conspirator, will save you.
You have wandered over land and sea,
now you will wander through the lower world,
a shadow even to the other shadows.
Though bloodless, you will bleed there.
Why don't you say something?
Are you laughing at us?
You will live to see us eat your living flesh,
you are a delicate dish especially cooked for us.

FURY 2

Watch us dance, listen to our consoling voice.
Did you know we were ministers of justice,

who cannot harm the innocent,
or even trouble his conscience? But you?
You have wronged the dead. In life or death,
I will not leave your side.

FURY 3

The mother of night is my mother—
why should the god of the sun oppose me?
Or pretend to save the coward trembling at the altar?
He was ours when he slew his mother.

FURY 1

Hear my song. I sing unaccompanied
by joy or any musical instrument,
except the invisible sizzling fires
that waste his demented spirit.

FURY 2

We will hunt him to the silent land;
he will not stand in his freedom there.
Whoever slays his kindred
will find us at his side.

FURY 3

His only comfort will be a wasting fire.

FURY 1

The immortal gods dare not interrupt our bloodfeast.
We did not wear white wedding garments,
when the heir of an ancient line
was slain in the heart of her household
by the hand of her child.
We chase that murderer,

waste him and wear him—
blood for blood,
new suffering for old wrong.

FURY 2

This duty is ours and no one else's;
the gods on Olympus cannot touch us,
for we are withdrawn from light and reason.
Despised, blood-dirty, barred
from the council and conversation of the gods,
how freely I leap on my prey.
My foot is hard, I have tripped the fugitive runner.
On earth he strutted in pride and glory.
His fate will be humble in the lower world,
where all life is diminished.

FURY 3

My black robe flutters about him, our feet dance.

FURY 2

I glide by him like a black and flashing cloud.

FURY 3

We can only live in the sunless dark.

FURY 1

Justice is fixed and grim.
We have the hands to achieve it.
We are queens
and do not forget the privileges of our office.
We are as deadly to the living as to the dead
we have already punished . . .

The condemned man neither sees nor knows
that we are at his side.

[*Enter* ATHENA]*

ATHENA

I heard you calling me.
I was far away walking by the Scamander,
and taking possession of the Trojan plunder
Agamemnon and the lesser Greek kings
allotted me, a third of all Troy.
I give it to Athens and Theseus her king.
I was tireless in coming here,
I flew on the winds instead of wings—
brilliant as the silver serpents on my breastplate.
Who is this man clinging in terror to my altar?
And these black old women waiting to hurt him?
I am not afraid of you. But who are you,
so unlike the gods or human women?
Stay where you are;
I will not condemn you for your ugliness.

FURY

We are furies—
one word is enough to tell you.
We are children of unending night.

ATHENA

I know your name and mother.

FURY

Soon you will have to respect our rights.
We chase murderers from their houses.

ATHENA

Can the fugitives never stop and rest?

FURY

Yes, in Hades' kingdom,
where they must give up hope of happiness.

ATHENA

And this man, is there no mercy for him?

FURY

He killed his mother.

ATHENA

Was it his duty, perhaps, to kill her?

FURY

A duty to kill a mother?

ATHENA

I have heard your plea,
I know nothing of his.

FURY

Nothing he says will weaken our testimony.

ATHENA

You are demanding vengeance not law.

FURY

Have you the skill to prove what you assert?
You too are unable to swerve from the truth . . .
Child of Zeus, we entrust our case to you.

ATHENA

You must accept our decision.

FURY

Child of Zeus, we will defer to you.

ATHENA

You are an unknown man, tell us
the names of your father and city.
What injustice has brought you here?
Or was it your crime? Face your accusers;
surely it's with reason you came here,
entered my temple, and dare clasp my image,
as if you held a floating plank on the sea.
You may have hope. Zeus pardoned
even Ixion who killed his mother's father
by digging a pit at dinner for the poor old man.
Speak well for yourself.

ORESTES

Lady Athena, do not look at me
as if I were a man guilty of blood.
My hands have not stained your image.
Religion says a murderer is cleansed
when the priest sprinkles him with the blood
of a suckling pig. This expiation I have made,
washed pure in many temples and long ago
by streams of water, streams of blood.
My father was Agamemnon, king of Argos,
the king of men who captained the great fleet,
and as your soldier crushed Troy

to a citiless mound of dust and smashed stone.
After ten years of battles, Agamemnon
sailed home from victory to his dishonored death.
O my loved Father,
your dark-spirited wife, my mother, trapped
you in a strong net. You could not move,
the water you trampled was red with your blood.
I was exiled, disinherited, yet managed
to return and kill her. I will not hide it;
it was blood for blood. Apollo threatened
me with inescapable tortures if I held back.
You must decide if I was right or wrong.

ATHENA

This case is too hard for man to judge;
even I cannot decide on blood-guilt
or what retribution must follow.
This too must be considered: that this man
came here freely, guiltless and purified.
I must receive him in my city as uncondemned.
Yet fate will not let me banish his enemies—
even if they fairly lose their cause,
the poison of their anger will infect us,
an incurable plague that rots like mist.
Whether they go or stay, the land will suffer.
Since chance has given me this trial,
I will choose twelve men, the best in Athens,
a jury set up forever for deciding murder.
They will discriminate between truth and falsehood,
and vote under oath.

[ATHENA *leaves*]

FURY

If the murderer can go free,
or the coward kill his mother,
then this precedent will depose
the old traditions and the ancient law.
Not only in apprehension then
will the parent die at the hands of his child.

FURY

The ruler will cry, "Look,
they are hurt, they fall, they die about me.
Is there no comfort?"

FURY

There is none.
The injured will ask requital of the furies.
We will not be there.

FURY

Cures will not heal.

FURY

Fear will be wisdom then and punish
long after we are gone.
The righteous will not be attended to,
only anger that no man can master.

FURY

Wisdom finds out the middle path;
he who errs to right or left,
by too little or too much, shall fall.

FURY

"I will not fall," the outlaw says, and falls.

FURY

He who follows his longings
will sail out of his seductive calm
and enter the day of storm
with lowered sail—
swallowed by the whirling waves.

FURY

Whatever happens, remember our words:
"Justice is your only safety."

[ATHENA *returns, with twelve* JURORS *and a* HERALD]*

ATHENA

Blow your trumpet, Herald,
and give it all your mortal breath,
warning us to sit in silence
until the jury have taken their seats.
May they judge wisely,
may Athens welcome this first trial by jury.

[APOLLO *enters*]*

FURY

Meddle with what is yours, Apollo,
you have no rights in our case.

APOLLO

I appear as witness for this man,
a guest and suppliant at my sacred temple,
there purified by me of blood-guilt.

I stand beside him at his trial,
as I stood beside him once in murder.

ATHENA

The hearing has opened. The furies,
as the plaintiffs, must speak first.

FURY

Though we are many, we'll need few words.
You must answer our questions word for word.
Do you confess you killed your mother?

ORESTES

I killed Clytemnestra. Why should I lie?

FURY

This is the first of three counts against you;
a third is death.

ORESTES

You have two to go, and are already gloating.

FURY

Tell us how you killed your mother.

ORESTES

I held her by the throat and struck.

FURY

Did any assurance or promise compel you?

ORESTES

The oracles of Apollo.

FURY

Did the holy prophet-god tell you to kill your mother?

ORESTES

Things went better for me because of him.

FURY

The jury will determine if things went better.

ORESTES

My great murdered father will come to protect me.

FURY

Is the killer of his mother reduced
to summoning ghosts?

ORESTES

Clytemnestra was doubly a betrayer.

FURY

You talk in riddles, speak clearly to the jury.

ORESTES

She killed her husband and my father.

FURY

Death frees her, while you still live under sentence.

ORESTES

Why didn't you track her down when she was living?

FURY

She was not blood-kin to her husband.

ORESTES

I am no kin to Clytemnestra.

FURY

How else were you born? You forswear your birth.

ORESTES

You must speak for me now, Apollo—
was her death good or evil?
I and my accusers wait.

APOLLO

I will plead correctly before your high court,
Athena. I ask for justice—
I, the prophet-god, who never cheated,
who never by a word slandered
man, woman or the State. Each sentence
I speak is determined by my father, Zeus.
When I expound, you hear Zeus.

FURY

You will say Zeus only avenges fathers—
that a mother is a thing to him, that his wife,
Hera the forgiver . . .

APOLLO

Agamemnon's death was not usual—
a king of kings crowned and sceptered by Zeus . . .
no life-despising Amazon arrowed him down
in the lines at Troy. Another kind of woman,
a coward and liar, betrayed him.
He was unarmed and helpless in his own house.
She laughed when she embraced him
in his unsuspecting pride and glory
trampling barefoot on the cloths she spread.
With her own hands, she washed his war-scarred body,
she netted him from head to foot.
He could never claw his way out

of the knotted loops that held him down.
How easy it was to kill a great king.

FURY

Is a father's murder the worst crime for Zeus?
He castrated his own father, the wise Cronos . . .
chained him and threw him in jail for life.
The justice of the gods is ambition.

APOLLO

How can monsters fed on anarchy and boredom
understand my father?
An imprisoned god can be released.
When men die, they die. They and you
will not escape the thirsty dust
already accumulating for your graves.
A ruler has no temptation to bend the law.

FURY

Do you mean that Orestes could only revere
Agamemnon by killing his mother?
Will the mother-killer walk in Argos
like Agamemnon,
and carelessly share the winebowl with his friends?

APOLLO

We run on. I will expound the law to you
and make my final argument.
The father not the mother is the parent.
Did you know a mother is only
a borrower, a nurse, a stranger who brings
a stranger's freshborn seed to life for him?
And for that the gods must favor her.

Do you want another reason?
What else could Orestes do . . .
exiled, disinherited, his father murdered?

I will say no more. Lady Athena,
no mother ever bore a fairer child
than you who sprang unmothered from god's brain.
Daughter of Zeus, resplendent shield of Athens,
my case is yours.

ATHENA

Enough has been said
for the jury to judge Orestes.

FURY

We have shot our arrows
and wait for the jury's confirmation.

ATHENA

[*To* ORESTES *and* APOLLO]
How shall I escape your reproach?

APOLLO

I have spoken very clearly;
the jury must be wise and remember their oath.

ATHENA

Here on this rock, the Areopagus,
where blood-guilt will first be judged by jury,
I give you my instructions. Juries
shall always meet on Ares' Hill—
here where the Amazons camped in tents
and sacrificed horses to the god of war,

and pitched wattled towers above our walls,
hoping to kill King Theseus and sack Athens.
Here awe and fear must press on the heart,
for untouched by fear no man is just.
Let no man serve tyrants or disobey law.
If the spring is fouled, you will not drink.
If you stand by law, you shall have a bulwark
no land can match, not Scythia or Sparta,
both famous in their day for justice.
Let this court, this jury be incorruptible,
swift to punish, awake to save those who sleep.

[*To the* JURY]

Take up your votes, think of your oath, be true.

[APOLLO *and the* FURIES *speak to the* JURY *as they cast their
votes one by one. Two urns receive the votes*]

FURY

I warn you—if you misjudge,
your city will suffer plagues from us.

APOLLO

Do you remember you heard me speak for Zeus?

FURY

Do not pretend you have Zeus' consent;
you have no authority over murder.

APOLLO

Zeus upheld Ixion, the first murderer.

FURY

Apollo twists our words . . . If we lose
we will come to your fields and blight them.

APOLLO

Shouldn't I save my unfortunate friend?

FURY

You young gods easily ride over us with words.
We're not the old gods you duped and bewildered with wine.
We wait for the jury. For their health,
may they keep our unanswered accusation in mind.

ATHENA

I tell you,
if the vote falls even, mine is for Orestes.
I wasn't given birth by a mother,
I owe no loyalty to women.
In all things, like Zeus my father,
I am a friend to man—
yet I shall never marry. It can't mean much
if a woman, who has killed her husband, is killed.
The vote is completed, the judges shall draw.

ORESTES

Now my life will end, O bright Apollo.

FURY

O black night, our mother, you must help us.

ORESTES

Now I must be hanged or live a king.

FURY

Now we shall win more power or our ruin.

APOLLO

Count your votes carefully. One you miscast
may mean a man's life or death.

ATHENA

The vote is six to six. I will make it
seven to six. Orestes
returns guiltless to Argos.

ORESTES

Athena, by your grace,
my house lives, and now you return me
to my father's land, once lost to me,
while I was mad and wandered. Now men
shall see a Greek lives in his father's house . . .
saved by Athena and Apollo, and by
one greater, Zeus the all-powerful.
He remembered my father and saved
me from strangling, he looked on
Clytemnestra's fiends and they were gone.
I journey home now, but first I swear,
"Now and for all time, no Argive leader
shall march his spearmen against Athens."
I shall long lie deep buried in the earth,
but if any violate my oath, I promise
I will bring sad adversities on him,
ill-starred journeys, roads to despair,
stratagems that recoil on the contriver . . .
Health now to those who keep my vow.
To Athens, farewell. May your hand's
grip be steady on your spear.

[ORESTES *exits.* APOLLO *exits*]*

FURIES

You evil young gods, why have you smashed
the old laws and torn them from our hands?

In sorrow we look for our inheritance,
and are angry. Blood drips from our hearts
to poison the fields of Athens.
No leaf shall grow now, herds shall be barren.
Why are we laughed at by the people?
Why are the sad daughters of the night dishonored?

ATHENA

You were never beaten, the vote was tied;
yet none can contest the will of Zeus,
or the pleas of Apollo, who both instigated
the murder and defended the murderer.
You must not strike this land with barrenness,
or send continual rain to flatten our crops.
You shall have a refuge with us, far underground,
and sit on shining chairs to be worshipped.

FURIES

No leaf shall grow now, herds shall be barren.
Why are the sad daughters of the night dishonored?

ATHENA

You were not dishonored. You will not make
this land uninhabited. I hold the keys of thunder;
you would not want to make me use them on you.
Let your black strength sleep,
come live with us and enjoy our land,
offerings for births and marriage-tithes.

FURIES

I am the mind of the past. Why do they treat
me so, and threaten to drive me underground?
Each breath I take is fury.

ATHENA

You are older and think yourselves wiser.
I must put up with you, yet Zeus gave me
an intelligence. If you go to another country,
you will wish yourselves back. Time fattens this city.
No other will give you such ceremonies,
if you do not drive our young men
to civil wars, like gamecocks
only jabbing for the heart,
blood-drunk, though sober.

FURY

I am the mind of the past. Why do they treat
me so, and threaten to drive me underground?

ATHENA

I'm not tired of selling you good things.
Old powers of darkness, you cannot complain
that a young Athena exiled you.
If you can believe persuasion's in my voice,
stay with us—then you'll not afflict your host.

FURY

What is this place you promised?

ATHENA

One without sorrow and yours.

FURY

If I take it, shall I have power?

ATHENA

No house will prosper without you.

FURY

Will I be stronger then?

ATHENA

Yes.

FURY

For a day or forever?

ATHENA

Now and always.

FURY

O queen, you are persuasion. I fear my hate is going.
What song shall I sing in praise of our Athens?

ATHENA

Say nothing of evil succeeding;
sing of the land, the Aegean,
mild breezes airing
a landscape shot with sunlight,
human seeds, all things that grow.
All's yours for the asking,
as a gardener works for love.

FURY

May the sun's brilliance break wave on wave—
all the happiness life can give this land.

ATHENA

Only these spirits hard to soften
can be trusted to manage man's life.
Ancient crimes shall drag the criminal

before the furies—
his voice is still loud, but the verdict silent.

FURIES

Let no wind blow to tear the trees—
singing for some, for others a life of tears.

APPENDIX

[Lowell made a draft of the first three scenes of *The Furies* in the 1960's, at the time he translated *Agamemnon* and *Orestes*. When he finally did a version of the entire play in 1976/7, he didn't consult—perhaps had forgotten—these pages. Two scenes are quite sketchy, decisively better in the complete version. The third is given below. I have bracketed one word; its transcription is uncertain. F.B.]

(The scene is the sanctuary of Apollo at Delphi)

PRIESTESS OF APOLLO

Peace to Apollo, peace to the gods,
who held dominion in Delphi before him
in the day of darkness. I honor the Earth,
her Daughter, Themis, and her Daughter, Phoebe.
Freedom not force installed them here.
Freedom not force sent us our Sun-god,
Phoebus Apollo, who sailed to Delphi
from Delos, first grounding his galley at Piraeus,
the port of Athens and Pallas Athena.
The sons of the fire-god, Hephaestus, helped him,
they leveled a roadbed through rock, and left
the wilderness a furrowed field.
Freedom not force, light not darkness,
free will and the will of Zeus, his Father,

gave us Apollo and [prophecy].
When I speak for Apollo, I speak for Zeus.

Listen, you will hear the hum of their voices
through the hush of these bald, bouldered hills.
Nymphs call once from the Corycian Rock,
birds sing in peace here, the bright
new gods brush by us. Bacchus pursues
the overprudent, Pentheus hooked like a hare
in the deathtrap.
I call on Zeus,* the Accomplisher. Listen,
springs ring, in the Gulf of Corinth,
the salt sea of Poseidon kicks
the white pebbles. These new gods
are merciless in their thirst for mercy.
Justice and light, but no letup for the helpless,
the old, the brittle. I will enter this temple,
may my entrance be the best in my life.
When I speak, Apollo will speak inside me.

    [*Several lines are missing here.*]

All about him, in front of him, behind him,
women snuggled on the temple benches.
No, they weren't women, I'd call them gorgons,
only they weren't gorgons. In a painting once,
I saw gorgons. They were scrabbling food
from King Phineus. Gorgons have wings, these don't.
Their skins and dresses were black as charcoal.
Their snoring made the flagstones tremble.

---

* *variant*: Athena

Snot mucked their eyes together,
and they weren't dressed properly to be in the presence
of the God's statue, or even to have inside
a human house. No people would welcome them,
no county confess to having borne them.

I've done what I could. I am terrified.
Oh Apollo, my healer, you know everything.
You can do everything. Save your servant!